Contents

Introduction

War & Conflict is Volume 401 in the **issues** series. The aim of the series is to offer current, diverse information about important issues in our world, from a UK perspective.

ABOUT WAR & CONFLICT

Regrettably, there is always a war going on somewhere in the world. This book explores the reasons for war, current and historic conflicts and various method of warfare. It also considers the consequences and victims of war, in particular the impact on children caught up in conflicts across the globe.

OUR SOURCES

Titles in the **issues** series are designed to function as educational resource books, providing a balanced overview of a specific subject.

The information in our books is comprised of facts, articles and opinions from many different sources, including:

♦ Newspaper reports and opinion pieces

♦ Website factsheets

♦ Magazine and journal articles

♦ Statistics and surveys

♦ Government reports

♦ Literature from special interest groups.

A NOTE ON CRITICAL EVALUATION

Because the information reprinted here is from a number of different sources, readers should bear in mind the origin of the text and whether the source is likely to have a particular bias when presenting information (or when conducting their research). It is hoped that, as you read about the many aspects of the issues explored in this book, you will critically evaluate the information presented.

It is important that you decide whether you are being presented with facts or opinions. Does the writer give a biased or unbiased report? If an opinion is being expressed, do you agree with the writer? Is there potential bias to the 'facts' or statistics behind an article?

ASSIGNMENTS

In the back of this book, you will find a selection of assignments designed to help you engage with the articles you have been reading and to explore your own opinions. Some tasks will take longer than others and there is a mixture of design, writing and research-based activities that you can complete alone or in a group.

FURTHER RESEARCH

At the end of each article we have listed its source and a website that you can visit if you would like to conduct your own research. Please remember to critically evaluate any sources that you consult and consider whether the information you are viewing is accurate and unbiased.

Useful Websites

www.bylinetimes.com

www.crisisgroup.org

www.icrc.org

www.inequality.com

www.independent.co.uk

www.owlcation.com

www.telegraph.co.uk

www.theconversation.com

www.theguardian.com

www.un.org

www.unherd.com

www.unicef.org

independence
educational publishers

First published by Independence Educational Publishers

The Studio, High Green

Great Shelford

Cambridge CB22 5EG

England

© Independence 2022

Copyright

Photocopy licence

ISBN-13: 978 1 86168 860 6

Printed in Great Britain

Zenith Print Group

The 8 main reasons for war

By Paul Goodman

What is a war?

A war is typically fought by a country or group of countries against an opposing country or group with the aim of achieving an objective through the use of force. Wars can also be fought within a country in the form of a civil or revolutionary war.

According to the *Oxford English Dictionary*, 'war' is defined as:

1. A state of armed conflict between different countries or different groups within a country.

2. A state of competition or hostility between different people or groups.

3. A sustained campaign against an undesirable situation or activity.

Wars have been a part of human history for thousands of years, and have become increasingly destructive as industrialization and technology have advanced.

What is the cause of conflict?

There is rarely one single, clear cause of conflict and, ultimately, war. The causes of a war are usually numerous and can often be intertwined in a complicated way.

Many theories have been put forth over the years as to why wars happen, and some of the greatest minds have offered their take on the subject.

In the article below, I'll provide a general overview of the eight main reasons for war. Given the many potential causes for conflict, the list does not attempt to be exhaustive, but does intend to give the most common reasons.

Eight main causes of war

1. Economic gain

Often wars are caused by one country's wish to take control of another country's wealth. Whatever the other reasons for a war may be, there is almost always an economic motive underlying most conflicts, even if the stated aim of the war is presented to the public as something more noble.

In pre-industrial times, the gains desired by a warring country might be precious materials such as gold and silver, or livestock such as cattle and horses.

In modern times, the resources that are hoped to be gained from war take the form of things like oil, minerals, or materials used in manufacturing.

Some scientists believe that as the world's population increases and basic resources become scarce, wars will be fought more often over fundamental essentials, such as water and food.

Historical examples of wars fought for economic gain

♦ **Anglo-Indian Wars (1766-1849)** – The Anglo-Indian wars were a series of wars fought between the British East India Company and different Indian states. These wars led to the establishment of British colonial rule in India, which gave Britain unrestricted access to exotic and valuable resources native to the Indian continent.

♦ **Finnish-Soviet War or 'The Winter War' (1939-1940)** – Stalin and his Soviet Army wanted to mine nickel in Finland, but when the Finnish refused, the Soviet Union waged war on the country.

2. Territorial gain

A country might decide that it needs more land, either for living space, agricultural use, or other purposes. Territory can also be used as 'buffer zones' between two hostile enemies.

Related to buffer zones are proxy wars. These are conflicts that are fought indirectly between opposing powers in a third country. Each power supports the side which best suits their logistical, military, and economic interests.

Proxy wars were particularly common during the Cold War.

Historical examples of wars fought for territorial gain

♦ **Mexican-American War (1846-1848)** – This war was fought following the annexation of Texas, with Mexico still claiming the land as their own. The U.S. outfought the Mexicans, retaining Texas and incorporating it as a state.

♦ **Serbo-Bulgarian War (1885-1886)** – Bulgaria and Serbia fought over a small border town after the river creating the border between the countries moved.

- ♦ **Arab-Israeli War or 'Six Day War' (1967-1988)** – Israeli forces took the territories of the West Bank, including East Jerusalem, from Jordan.

3. Religion

Religious conflicts often have very deep roots. They can lie dormant for decades, only to re-emerge in a flash at a later date.

Religious wars can often be tied to other reasons for conflict, such as nationalism or revenge for a perceived historical slight in the past.

While different religions fighting against each other can be a cause of war, different sects within a religion (for example, Protestant and Catholic, or Sunni and Shiite) battling against one another can also instigate war.

Historical examples of wars fought for religion

The Crusades (1095-1291) – The Crusades were a series of wars sanctioned by the Latin Church during the medieval age. The aim of crusaders was to expel Islam and spread Christianity.

Thirty Years' War (1618-1648) – When Holy Roman Emperor Ferdinand II tried to impose Roman Catholicism on the people of his domains, a faction of Protestants from the north banded together, sparking war.

Lebanese Civil War (1975-1990) – The Lebanese Civil War was primarily sparked from conflicts between the Sunni Muslim, Shiite Muslim and Christian Lebanese populations.

Yugoslav Wars (1991-1995) – The Yugoslav wars consisted of the Croatian War and the Bosnian War. The wars were fought between the orthodox Catholic and Muslim populations of former Yugoslavia.

Second Sudanese Civil War (1983-2005) – This ethnoreligious war was caused by the Muslim central government's choice to impose Sharia law on non-muslim southerners.

4. Nationalism

Nationalism in this context essentially means attempting to prove that your country is superior to another by violent subjugation. This often takes the form of an invasion.

Dr. Richard Ned Lebow, Professor of International Political Theory at the Department of War Studies, Kings College London, contends that while other causes of war may be present, nationalism, or spirit, is nearly always a factor. In his essay 'Most wars are not fought for reasons of security or material interests, but instead reflect a nation's spirit,' he writes:

'Literature on war and its causes assumes security is the principal motive of states and insecurity the major cause of war. Following Plato and Aristotle, I posit spirit, appetite and reason as fundamental drives with distinct goals. There can be little doubt that the spirit is the principal cause of war across the centuries.'

Related to nationalism is imperialism, which is built on the idea that conquering other countries is glorious and brings honour and esteem to the conqueror.

Racism can also be linked to nationalism, as can be seen in Hitler's Germany. Adolf Hitler went to war with Russia partly because the Russians (and eastern Europeans in general) were seen as Slavs, or a group of people who the Nazis believed to be an inferior race.

Historical examples of wars fought for nationalism

Chichimeca War (1550-1590) – The Chichimeca war was one of many wars fought during the Spanish conquest of the Aztec civilization in modern day Mexico.

World War I (1914-1918) – Extreme loyalty and patriotism caused many countries to become involved in the first world war. Many pre-war Europeans believed in the cultural, economic and military supremacy of their nation.

5. Revenge

Seeking to punish, redress a grievance, or simply strike back for a perceived slight can often be a factor in the waging of war. Revenge also relates to nationalism, as the people of a country which has been wronged are motivated to fight back by pride and spirit.

Unfortunately, this can lead to an endless chain of retaliatory wars being set in motion which is very difficult to stop.

Historically, revenge has been a factor in many European wars.

Historical examples of wars fought for revenge

World War II (1939-1945) – The rise of the Nazi Socialist Party and Germany's eventual domination of the European continent were direct results of the Treaty of Versailles, which imposed strict punishments on Germany.

War on Terror – The September 11th attacks on the World Trade Center in 2001 prompted President George W. Bush to initiate a war on terror. This global war began with an invasion of Iraq and is ongoing.

6. Civil War

These generally take place when there is sharp internal disagreement within a country.

The disagreement can be about who rules, how the country should be run or the people's rights. These internal rifts often turn into chasms that result in violent conflict between two or more opposing groups.

Civil wars can also be sparked by separatist groups who want to form their own, independent country, or, as in the case of the American Civil War, states wanting to secede from a larger union.

Historical examples of civil wars

American Civil War (1861-1865) - The American Civil War was fought by the Union army and the Confederate army as a result of the long-standing controversy over slavery.

Russian Civil War (1917-1923) – The Russian Civil War followed immediately after the Russian Revolution, with the Red Army and the White Army vying to determine Russia's political future.

Spanish Civil War (1936-1939) – The Spanish Civil War was fought between the Republicans, who were loyal to the left-leaning Second Spanish Republic, and the Nationalists, a largely aristocratic conservative group led by General Francisco Franco.

Korean War (1950-1953) – The Korean War was a war fought between North Korea, which was supported by China, and South Korea, which was supported primarily by the United States.

7. Revolutionary War

These occur when a large section of the population of a country revolts against the individual or group that rules the country because they are dissatisfied with their leadership.

Revolutions can begin for a variety of reasons, including economic hardship amongst certain sections of the population or perceived injustices committed by the ruling group. Other factors can contribute too, such as unpopular wars with other countries.

Revolutionary wars can easily descend into civil wars.

Historical examples of revolutionary wars

Portuguese Restoration War (1640-1668) – The Portuguese revolution ended the 60-year rule of Portugal by Spain.

American Revolution (1775-1783) – The American Revolution gave the 13 North American colonies independence from British rule and established the United States of America.

French Revolution (1789-1799) – The French Revolution was a battle that represented the rise of the bourgeoisie and the downfall of the aristocracy in France.

Haitian Revolution (1791-1804) – The Haitian Revolution was a successful slave rebellion that established Haiti as the first free black republic.

8. Defensive War

In the modern world, where military aggression is more widely questioned, countries will often argue that they are fighting in a purely defensive capacity against an aggressor, or potential aggressor, and that their war is therefore a 'just' war.

These defensive wars can be especially controversial when they are launched preemptively, the argument essentially being that: 'We are attacking them before they inevitably attack us.'

Historical examples of defensive wars

Iraqi Conflict (2003-Present) – An international coalition, led by the US, invaded Iraq on the grounds that the country's leader, Saddam Hussein, was developing weapons of mass destruction, and therefore presented a threat to surrounding countries and rest of the world. The war was controversial as the allegations made about the weapons of mass destruction made by the US and UK were shown to lack substance.

18 April 2021

Wars without end: why is there no peaceful solution to so much global conflict?

A new study shows that 60% of the world's wars have lasted for at least a decade. From Afghanistan to Libya, Syria to Congo DRC, has endless conflict become normalised?

By Simon Tisdall

Libya's civil war entered its 7th year this month with no end in sight. In Afghanistan, conflict has raged on and off since the Soviet invasion in 1979. America's Afghan war is now its longest ever, part of the open-ended US 'global war on terror' launched after the 2001 al-Qaida attacks.

Yemen's conflict is in its sixth pitiless year. In Israel-Palestine, war – or rather the absence of peace – has characterised life since 1948. Somalis have endured 40 years of fighting. These are but a few examples in a world where the idea of war without end seems to have become accepted, even normalised.

Why do present-day politicians, generals, governments and international organisations appear incapable or uninterested in making peace? In the 19th and 20th centuries, broadly speaking, wars commenced and concluded with formal ultimatums, declarations, agreed protocols, truces, armistices and treaties.

Neat and tidy endings, even if sometimes illusory, are rarer these days. According to a survey published last week by the International Institute for Strategic Studies, 60% of armed conflicts have been active for at least a decade and peace-making prospects globally are in decline.

Today's wars are mostly undeclared, undefined and inglorious affairs typically involving multiple parties, foreign governments, proxy forces, covert methods and novel weapons. They are conducted without regard for civilian lives, the Geneva conventions regulating armed conflict, or the interests of host populations in whose name they are fought.

Great moral crusades, famous causes and genuine ideological struggles are few and far between. Modern wars are mostly about power and treasure. And they go on, and on, and on.

Libya is a classic case of a state of chaos deliberately fed and manipulated by external powers, in this instance Turkey, Qatar, Russia, Egypt and the UAE. Here, as elsewhere, rival rulers claim to be upholding order or fighting 'terrorism' while, in reality, they seek to extend national influence and economic advantage. As long as these aims remain unmet, they show scant interest in peace.

Ambitious states have always sought to dominate neighbours in the way China, for example, is doing now. One reason this happens more frequently today, and more anarchically, is declining American engagement.

In the Middle East and Africa, the US – no longer a global policeman – is focused on supporting Israel, squeezing Iran and selling arms, to the exclusion of almost all else. In Asia, it is in retreat.

Donald Trump, desperate for a Nobel peace prize, offered to mediate the 70-year-old North Korea-South Korea stand-off. He also claims his 'deal of the century' will solve the Israel-Palestine conundrum. Few take him seriously. Otherwise, his administration has shown zero interest in global conflict resolution.

A related factor is the collapse of the western-led consensus favouring multilateral, collaborative approaches to international problems. This is matched by the parallel rise of authoritarian and populist regimes that prioritise narrow national interest over perceptions of the common good.

This trend, a regression to the pre-1914 era of competing European nation-states, undermines the authority of the UN and cooperative regional platforms such as the EU and African Union. Unsupported, UN peace envoys from Syria to Myanmar and peacekeeping operations across Africa struggle to make headway.

Ineffective international law enforcement, symbolised by the inability of the International Criminal Court to deliver justice to war zones such as Iraq and Ukraine, helps freeze or perpetuate conflicts rather than justly resolve them. Demographic and physical causes also contribute to chronic instability.

Conflict in the Democratic Republic of Congo, the Sahel and Sudan is fuelled by the fact that millions of young men in Africa, where the median age is 19.8, lack fulfilling work or a meaningful stake in their country's future. Long-running inter-state or intra-state violence is also rooted in the climate crisis and resulting resource scarcity, poverty and dislocation.

New technologies and weapons such as drones and cyber warfare are lowering the up-front cost of conflict while enlarging potential theatres of war. Global warming is turning the newly accessible Arctic into a vast, pristine battleground. Outer space presents infinite possibilities for violence.

Religious wars are often the most bitterly fought and hardest to halt. As in the past, multiple collisions of faith, culture and values between Christians, Jews, Muslims, Hindus and other belief systems are key elements in the early 21st century's insatiable addiction to war.

The Muslim world is also divided internally, between the Shia and Sunni traditions and fundamentalist and secular interpretations of Islam. These schisms have been depicted by the Arabic noun fitna, which can mean both 'charm, enchantment, captivation' and 'rebellion, riot, discord, civil strife'.

Fitna is a fitting word for describing not only the Islamic sphere but the troubled state of the world as a whole in 2020, beset as it is by wars without end. For many people, if they are honest, war has a fatal attraction. As WB Yeats noted after the 1916 Easter Rising in Ireland, violent conflict

4

can spawn a 'terrible beauty' – a mix of fascination and horror that is difficult to forswear.

Syria

War began: March 2011

An initially peaceful uprising against the autocratic presidency of Bashar al-Assad formed part of the 2011 Arab Spring revolts. It quickly turned into full-scale war as Assad's regional foes, notably Saudi Arabia, seized a chance to overthrow a regime allied with Iran. Since then upwards of half a million people are estimated to have died.

The US and Europe also sought to install a friendly, pro-western government in Damascus. As Assad's grip on power weakened, Russia, supported by Iran, intervened in 2015 to stave off collapse and thwart western ambitions. Other interventions came from Turkey and from Islamic State jihadists, who declared a caliphate in Syria and Iraq.

The war continues in the north-western province of Idlib, the last rebel-held stronghold, to which millions have fled. A current ceasefire is not expected to last. There are also fears that up to 100,000 people could die there if Covid-19 spreads in crowded refugee camps. Dr Munzer al-Khalil, head of Idlib's health directorate said: 'If we do not get more support and equipment, we know we will not be able to cope. The people of north-west Syria have been through enough. We need the WHO to help and to help fast.'

Afghanistan

War began: September 2001

The US invasion initially aimed to kill or capture the al-Qaida terrorists responsible for the 9/11 attacks. But it quickly expanded into a 'regime change' operation tasked with eliminating the Taliban and creating a functioning, democratic state.

Those latter objectives have proved unattainable despite large deployments of US, British and Nato troops and expenditure totalling billions of dollars. The elected Afghan government remains weak and divided, while the Taliban are resurgent. Pakistani, Indian, Iranian and Russian interference is a constant problem.

The US is now seeking to cut its losses and leave. But a controversial 'peace deal' has failed to take hold. It is widely viewed as a mere fig-leaf for an American troop withdrawal intended to boost Donald Trump's re-election chances.

At least 100,000 Afghans are estimated to have died since 2001, although the true figure, including deaths from indirect causes, is almost certainly much higher. According to the UN, Afghan forces and their US allies caused more civilian casualties in 2019 than the Taliban. With Isis terrorists now regularly launching attacks, hopes of peace are fading.

Libya

War began: May 2014

Turmoil in Libya actually began in October 2011 when the dictator Muammar Gaddafi was overthrown in a popular revolt backed by the UK, France and the US. But national celebrations were short-lived.

A power struggle between myriad political factions, tribes, militias, and jihadists brought an open rupture in 2014 between the UN-backed government in Tripoli and dissenting parliamentarians who re-based themselves in Tobruk to the east.

Foreign powers with an interest in Libya's oil and strategic orientation have since weighed in, with Egypt, the UAE and Russia backing eastern armed forces under General Khalifa Haftar, a self-styled strongman who claims to be fighting Islamist terrorism. Ranged against him is the Tripoli government supported by Turkey, Qatar and some European states. Both Moscow and Ankara have reportedly sent mercenaries to support rival sides. Last week the US claimed Russia was supplying Haftar with warplanes.

The chaos prevalent in much of Libya's contested and ungoverned spaces has been exploited by people, arms and drug traffickers. To the consternation of Italy and the EU, the country has become a Mediterranean stepping-off point for northwards migration. UN-backed peace efforts are at a standstill.

Yemen

War began: March 2015

The war in Yemen, already a grievously disadvantaged country, has helped create what the UN describes as the world's worst humanitarian disaster. Fighting has compounded perils posed by extreme poverty, malnutrition, cholera, climate change, religious extremism and now, Covid-19.

A ceasefire arranged as a result of the pandemic ended last month despite UN efforts to advance a peace process. Now the war seems to be escalating again, with new missile attacks reported last week. More than 40,000 people have fled their homes since January, adding to the 3.6 million displaced. Unicef says 12 million children need humanitarian assistance.

The impasse owes much to the fact the main protagonists – the Yemeni government, led by exiled president Abd Rabbu Mansour Hadi, and the Houthi rebel movement, which represents Yemen's Zaidi Shia minority – are backed by regional rivals Saudi Arabia and Iran respectively. The Saudi military intervened in 2015 after Hadi was forced to flee, backed by the US, UK and France. But while civilian casualties and alleged war crimes have rocketed, the Houthi insurgency appears largely unscathed. Meanwhile, al-Qaida terrorists are exploiting the chaos and southern separatists based in Aden have gained ground.

Democratic Republic of Congo

War began: 1997

It's hard to say exactly when the trouble began in the DRC. This vast central African country experienced an extraordinary civil war between 1997 and 2003 when an estimated five million people died. Continuing instability in lawless areas of north-eastern DRC bordering Uganda stems from that period.

International concern about an ebola outbreak in Goma, the main eastern city, has been overtaken by worries about Covid-19. Meanwhile, violence involving numerous armed groups is remorseless. At least 40 villagers were killed in recent machete attacks by the Allied Democratic Forces, a renegade militia claiming links to Isis.

About 400 people have died in Ituri province at the hands of the ADF since last year. UN peacekeepers are unable to stop the violence. And, unlike in other conflict zones, western countries are not keen to get involved. The Norwegian Refugee Council says that, overall, more than 480,000 people have been displaced in DRC since March when the UN appealed for a global ceasefire.

31 May 2020

'Almost divine power': the lawyers who sign off who lives and who dies in modern war zones

An article from the *The Conversation*.

THE CONVERSATION

By Craig Jones, Lecturer in Political Geography, @thewarspace, Newcastle University

When we think of war, we might think of soldiers on the front line – or those pulling the trigger – as the ones responsible for the death or injuries of those they are targeting. But my research suggests that over the past few decades an unlikely profession has become deeply involved in the conduct of war: lawyers.

Legal advisers (also called military lawyers) are trained as soldiers and are also qualified lawyers. It's a military lawyer's job to interpret the myriad rules of war, weigh the legal risk of a proposed action and provide preferably pithy advice and a range of lawful options for military activities to harried commanders. This could include guidance on the type of weapons that should be used, the timing of an attack to reduce the risk of casualties, or whether commanders should hold off and wait for more intelligence before proceeding.

State militaries have employed lawyers for decades – even centuries. But since the start of the 'war on terror' in 2001, military lawyers have played an increasingly vital role in deciding who lives and who dies in modern conflict zones.

I spent several years interviewing military lawyers at various locations in the Middle East, Europe and North America – from military bases, bustling cafes and even their own homes and gardens. They spoke candidly about how commanders had come to rely on their legal advice in lethal military operations, but also about their unease as lawyers in wielding this newfound power and the impact it has on their mental health.

Legal advisers told me how they often find themselves in situations where they are called into operations rooms in the middle of the night, asked to rapidly review the situation and give their bottom line.

One described being 'the sole remaining impediment to a sentence of death'. And although military lawyers receive specific training before being assigned to roles, my research suggests it's not always sufficient to prepare them for the highly stressful work of effectively advising on who should live and who should die in war zones.

'Getting humans to kill'

Legal advisers are not decision-makers: their job is to advise. It remains the responsibility of military commanders to decide, for example, whether or not a strike goes ahead. But from my research, it seems that in many instances, commanders sometimes look to lawyers for something approximating permission, or even psychological and moral support, as well as for legal advice.

One military lawyer described to me how his advice seemed to have an 'almost divine power' that could cause commanders to hesitate or to depart from their intuition. Another lawyer wrote about the reality of the power he holds:

I, as the legal advisor, am being asked by the commander whether he may legally kill these humans. I am the judge – he the jury and executioner.

Another lawyer disclosed to me that he felt 'more like a chaplain than a lawyer' because commanders came to him not only for legal advice but also for moral absolution. While another lawyer told me that his legal support was a vital component in 'getting human beings to ... kill other human beings in the name of the state'.

Advice under pressure

The US first pioneered the use of legal advisers in aerial targeting operations in the early 1990s. But now many other nations, including Israel, the UK, Australia, Canada, France and the Netherlands, along with other NATO member states, regularly consult legal experts before, during and after launching military strikes.

My research focuses specifically on the US and Israel and looks at the extent to which legal advisers are involved in various stages of aerial targeting – known colloquially as the 'kill chain' – a process whereby a target is identified, tracked and ultimately killed or destroyed.

In recent decades, as surveillance technologies have become more sophisticated and widespread, the kill chain has been compressed. A process that once took several weeks (and sometimes months) can take place, in theory, in hours and minutes. This means that military lawyers often operate in high-pressure environments – where there is no real time for deliberation or second opinions.

And sometimes military lawyers and commanders get it wrong. Like in 2016, when heavily armed US aircraft repeatedly fired on a hospital run by aid organisation Médecins Sans Frontières in Afghanistan thinking it was an enemy building. Or in 2002, when the Israel Air Force killed thirteen civilians in Gaza, including eight children, with a one-tonne bomb meant for a single military leader. On another occasion in Gaza, more than 20 members of one family were killed in a single strike.

In fact, a study by the non-profit organisation Human Rights Watch found that time-sensitive targeting operations tend to cause more civilian casualties than pre-planned operations – where more time is available for decision making.

The wrong target

I wanted to learn more about the real-world consequences of aerial targeting and legal advice. What did it look like on the ground to those beneath the barrage of bombs? So as part of my research, I also spoke to several people who had lost family members and their homes as a result of military airstrikes.

In one well-documented strike in Mosul, Iraq, in 2015, an innocent civilian, Basim Razzo, lost his whole family to a military strike orchestrated by the US and executed by the Dutch Air Force as part of the war against Islamic State.

The US military claimed the 'target' was an Islamic State compound producing car bombs, but in reality, it was two homes – one where Basim lived with his wife, Mayada, and daughter, Tuqa, and adjacent, another where his brother, Mohannad, lived with his wife, Azza, and son, Najib. Basim was the sole survivor and following lengthy investigations the US military offered him US$15,000 (£10,600) as compensation – which he refused.

I spoke to Basim in April 2019, over three and a half years later. He told me how difficult day-to-day life still was. He suffers from chronic pain and has had several surgeries. He's unable to work and earn a living because of his ongoing injuries, and he grieves the loss of his family.

As Basim put it, 'there are no words to describe what happened to me'. Five years after the attack and still unable to walk or work, the Dutch government eventually made a 'voluntary offer' of compensation to Basim, which he accepted.

Haunted by advice

Given the implications of their work, accounts are beginning to emerge – perhaps unsurprisingly – that some military lawyers are haunted by moral injury and post-traumatic stress disorder (PTSD).

Then there's also the issue that when military lawyers give advice that commanders don't want to hear, they are often told to 'stay in their lane'. As one lawyer told me, his advice should 'maximise the space for the commander to make a decision' – but sometimes that advice goes unheard.

And herein lies the problem, the boundaries of the law, porous though they are, might temporarily demarcate the space of allowable violence, but it is not always helpful for navigating right from wrong – particularly when it concerns the decision to end human life.

12 May 2021

Like in 1914 or 1939, we may be sleepwalking towards a global war that nothing can stop

There are lessons from previous conflicts that could prevent another from starting, but they are not all reassuring ones.

By Robert Tombs

Catastrophe can come out of the blue. Shortly before Britain was dragged into the devastating French revolutionary wars, the then prime minister William Pitt reassured the House of Commons that 'there never was a time in the history of this country when ... we might more reasonably expect fifteen years of peace.' In 1938, Neville Chamberlain won global plaudits for securing 'peace for our time'. In 1914, just before the German army marched in, the French public was wholly absorbed by the trial of a politician's wife who had killed an indiscreet journalist. (She got off.)

Might future generations wonder how we in our turn could be so focused on omicron and apparently illegal Christmas parties while Russian armies mustered, the Chinese airforce menaced Taiwan, and Iran stood on the brink of making the nuclear weapons that Israel had sworn it would never permit?

There are lessons from these past disasters, not all of them encouraging.

First is that a potential disturber of the peace must think that it can win – but so must those resisting it. No one, however unbalanced, embarks on a conflict they expect to lose. The weaker side backs down.

As long as the United States was clearly predominant – which it generally has been since 1945 – there would be no direct Great Power clash. It is when the balance of power becomes uncertain that danger arises, because both sides can anticipate victory.

Nuclear weapons for a time seemed to have changed the rules, but only if it is credible that they would be used. Now it is not.

Second, aggressors must think that they can win quickly and at acceptable cost – 'over by Christmas' is the fatal illusion, often coloured by ideology.

In 1792, both the French revolutionaries and their monarchical enemies were confident of a rapid walk-over. The former trusted in revolutionary fervour; the latter in professional discipline. In 1914, both sides had planned a quick and decisive campaign. In 1940, Hitler expected the decadent British to make peace, the materialistic Americans to stay neutral, and the inferior Russians to collapse. In both cases Germany's rulers knew that they would lose a long war.

Third, and perhaps most dangerous, is when a potential aggressor thinks that time is running out. Since 1870, Germany had been a rising force, economically, culturally, and militarily, and so its rulers saw no reason to seek trouble.

But by the 1900s, the country's rise had stalled, and Germany's chances of becoming one of the leading world powers was slipping away. Its rivals seemed to be 'encircling' it, and preparing for war. The German army and its Austrian allies believed in 1914 that they could still win, and quickly; but only for another couple of years.

The Nazis similarly believed that their time was running out, and that only bold and decisive action could save them.

If you think conflict is inevitable, logic means you act fast, whatever the risk. As the Austrian chief-of-staff put it chillingly in 1914, 'now we play va banque'. Hitler used the same gambling metaphor in 1939.

None of this is reassuring. Today, Russia is still powerful, but in decline. China until recently appeared to be in unstoppable ascent. But now its economy is stalling, its population ageing, and (like Germany before 1914) it has alarmed its rivals. Its rulers may be starting to feel 'encircled' as America, Japan, India and now Britain start to react.

If Russia wants another slice of Ukraine, it may not have long to grab it. And if China wants Taiwan, both for prestige and for its semiconductor industry, its chances may not be improving. As for Iran, is it already too late for it to develop usable nuclear weapons, or will it rush to do so while its enemies hesitate? Who might play va banque?

Could past generations have staved off the disasters of 1792, 1914 and 1939? Even with hindsight, there seem no simple solutions, no moment at which any politically feasible action could have saved the world.

Take the most notorious case, the Munich Conference of 1938, when Chamberlain made a last attempt to 'appease' Germany. We now know that had France and Britain gone to war, Germany would have been fighting a losing battle and its generals would probably have overthrown Hitler.

Disaster averted? But the peoples of Britain, France, the Empire and the United States were not then reconciled to fighting for Czechoslovakia, 'a faraway country of which we know nothing'. Chamberlain's concession was almost universally, even hysterically, praised.

If we venture into political science fiction, we have a little more scope. The best chance of preventing these three global wars would have been a broad alliance – strictly defensive, but clearly willing and able to resist aggression. To deter the French revolutionaries, an alliance based on Britain, Prussia and Austria. To deter the Kaiser and Hitler, an alliance of France, Britain, and Russia, and with the United States, already the potential superpower, prepared to intervene.

These alliances, which eventually came into being as a result of those wars, would have been the best chance of preventing them if they had existed before conflict broke out. That was impossible then, because of deep mistrust between the powers, and because of America's determined isolationism – always tempting for a country which can be self- sufficient if it has to be.

But what was impossible in 1791, 1913 and 1938 may not be impossible today. Indeed, Nato is precisely this kind of defensive alliance. Involving America in the relations between the major states has been the core of Britain's international strategy since 1940, indeed perhaps since 1916; and in the end it worked. At least until now.

The first aim of the democracies must be to prevent fatal miscalculation by potential aggressors: to convince them that they cannot win quickly and at low cost. Conflict delayed may be conflict averted, if potential aggressors come to accept that their 'window of opportunity' has closed.

This of course is basic deterrence. Hopefully, the rulers of Russia and China are less ideologically driven and hence more rational than the revolutionaries of 1792, the racists of 1939 or even the social darwinists of 1914.

Must there be carrots as well as sticks? The danger is that conciliation is hard to distinguish from 'appeasement', and may encourage aggression.

One advantage we have over earlier generations is that we can communicate more effectively with the peoples of hostile states, in a way the diplomats of 1914 would scarcely have contemplated. The democracies must show the peoples of Russia, China and Iran that we are not their enemies.

We have to trust that our highest values are of universal appeal, and not just a 'Western' peculiarity. For that, we need to regain the confidence to speak not just for ourselves, but for people everywhere.

31 December 2021

War profiteering is real. We need to end it

CEOs of major military contractors enjoyed a big jump in the value of their personal stock holdings after the U.S. airstrike that killed an Iranian military leader.

By Sarah Anderson

The prospect of war with Iran is terrifying.

Experts predict as many as a million people could die if the current tensions lead to a full-blown war. Millions more would become refugees across the Middle East, while working families across the U.S. would bear the brunt of our casualties.

But there is one set of people who stand to benefit from the escalation of the conflict: CEOs of major U.S. military contractors.

This was evident in the immediate aftermath of the U.S. assassination of a top Iranian military official on January 2. As soon as the news reached financial markets, these companies' share prices spiked.

Wall Street traders know that a war with Iran would mean more lucrative contracts for U.S. weapons makers. Since top executives get much of their compensation in the form of stock, they benefit personally when the value of their company's stock goes up.

I took a look at the stock holdings of the CEOs at the top five Pentagon contractors (Lockheed Martin, Boeing, General Dynamics, Raytheon, and Northrop Grumman).

Using the most recent available data, I calculated that these five executives held company stock worth approximately $319 million just before the U.S. drone strike that killed Iranian leader Qasem Soleimani. By the stock market's closing bell the following day, the value of their combined shares had increased to $326 million.

War profiteering is nothing new. Back in 2006, during the height of the Iraq War, I analyzed CEO pay at the 34 corporations that were the top military contractors at that time. I found that their pay had jumped considerably after the September 11 attacks.

Between 2001 and 2005, military contractor CEO pay jumped 108 percent on average, compared to a 6 percent increase for their counterparts at other large U.S. companies.

Congress needs to take action to prevent a catastrophic war on Iran. De-escalating the current tensions is the most immediate priority.

But Congress must also take action to end war profiteering. In 2008, John McCain, then a Republican presidential candidate, proposed capping CEO pay at companies receiving financial bailouts. He argued that CEOs relying on taxpayer funds should not earn more than $400,000 – the salary of the U.S. president.

That commonsense notion should be extended to all companies that rely on massive taxpayer-funded contracts. Senator Bernie Sanders, for instance, has a plan to deny federal contracts to companies that pay their CEOs excessively. He would set the CEO pay limit for major contractors at no more than 150 times the pay of the company's typical worker.

Currently, the sky's the limit for CEO pay at these companies – and the military contracting industry is a prime offender. The top five Pentagon contractors paid their top executives $22.5 million on average in 2018.

CEO pay restrictions should also apply to the leaders of privately held government contractors, which currently don't even have to disclose the size of their top executives' paychecks.

That's the case for General Atomics, the manufacturer of the MQ-9 Reaper that carried out the assassination of Soleimani. Despite raking in $2.8 billion in taxpayer-funded contracts in 2018, the drone maker is allowed to keep executive compensation information secret.

We do know that General Atomics CEO Neal Blue has prospered quite a bit from taxpayer dollars. Forbes estimates his wealth at $4.1 billion.

War is bad for nearly everyone. But as long as we allow the leaders of our privatized war economy to reap unlimited rewards, their profit motive for war in Iran – or anywhere – will persist.

13 January 2020

This op-ed was distributed by OtherWords. Sarah Anderson directs the Global Economy Project at the Institute for Policy Studies and co-edits Inequality.org. Follow her at @SarahDAnderson1

Can history teach us anything about the future of war – and peace?

A decade on from psychologist Steven Pinker's declaration that violence is declining, historians show no sign of agreeing a truce.

By Laura Spinney

Ten years ago, the psychologist Steven Pinker published *The Better Angels of Our Nature,* in which he argued that violence in almost all its forms – including war – was declining. The book was ecstatically received in many quarters, but then came the backlash, which shows no signs of abating. In September, 17 historians published a riposte to Pinker, suitably entitled *The Darker Angels of Our Nature,* in which they attacked his 'fake history' to 'debunk the myth of non-violent modernity'. Some may see this as a storm in an intellectual teacup, but the central question – can we learn anything about the future of warfare from the ancient past? – remains an important one.

Pinker thought we could and he supported his claim of a long decline with data stretching thousands of years back into prehistory. But among his critics are those who say that warfare between modern nation states, which are only a few hundred years old, has nothing in common with conflict before that time, and therefore it's too soon to say if the supposed 'long peace' we've been enjoying since the end of the second world war is a blip or a sustained trend.

In 2018, for example, computer scientist Aaron Clauset of the University of Colorado Boulder crunched data on wars fought between 1823 and 2003 and concluded that we'd have to wait at least another century to find out. Clauset doesn't think it would help to add older data into the mix; indeed, he thinks it would muddy the picture.

'It's up to researchers who study sub-state-level violence to substantiate their claims that the dynamics of such violence are relevant to the dynamics of war and, in my view, they haven't done a great job there,' he says.

Most researchers accept that there is a difference between war and interpersonal violence – and that these two things are governed by different forces – but there is disagreement over where to draw the line between them. Historian and archaeologist Ian Morris of Stanford University, author of *War! What Is it Good For?* (2014), is among those who say

that the nature of collective violence hasn't changed much in millennia, it's just that human groups were smaller in the past. For him, therefore, a massacre of a couple of dozen of hunter-gatherers in Sudan around about 13,000 years ago, the earliest known example of collective violence, is relevant to a discussion of modern warfare.

Archaeologist Detlef Gronenborn of the Römisch-Germanisches Zentralmuseum in Mainz, Germany, agrees. In 2015, he and others described a massacre among Europe's earliest farmers at a place called Schöneck-Kilianstädten in Germany, about 7,000 years ago. More than two dozen individuals were killed by blunt force instruments or arrows and dumped in a mass grave, their lower legs having been systematically broken either just before or just after death. The absence of young women from the group suggested that the attackers may have kidnapped them. Gronenborn says that massacres of entire communities were frequent occurrences in Europe at that time and that one of their hallmarks, judging by the human remains, was the desire to erase the victims' identity. 'The only difference between then and now is that of scale,' he says.

But while some researchers may agree with Pinker that prehistoric and modern warfare are essentially the same phenomenon, they don't necessarily agree with him that the evidence points to a long-term decline. Pinker based his claim that prehistory was extremely violent on around 20 archaeological sites spanning 14,000 years. Those sites unequivocally attest to ancient violence, says historian Dag Lindström of Uppsala University in Sweden, 'but they cannot be used for quantitative comparative conclusions'. We simply have no way of knowing how representative they were.

'The further you go back in time, the more difficult it becomes to have an accurate assessment of how many people died in battle,' says historian Philip Dwyer of the University of Newcastle in Australia, who co-edited *The Darker Angels of Our Nature.* Civilian death counts are even less reliable, he says, and have likely been significantly underestimated throughout history. In Dwyer's view, all war-related statistics are suspect, undermining attempts to identify long-term trends.

Others think the statistics can be informative. Gronenborn's work is feeding into larger scale efforts to identify and explain patterns in collective violence. One such effort is the Historical Peace Index (HPI), a collaboration between Oxford University and the group behind Seshat: Global History Databank – a scientific research project of the nonprofit Evolution Institute – to map warfare globally over the past 5,000 years. Their goal, as the name suggests, is to try to understand the causes and consequences of war, with a view to building more peaceful and stable societies.

The argument of those taking this kind of approach is that the more data you gather, the more you can identify meaningful patterns. Gronenborn, for example, says that it is beginning to look as if collective violence was cyclical in neolithic Europe. One hypothesis he and others are testing is that mounting internal social tensions fuelled explosions of violence, with external shocks such as climate fluctuations acting as triggers.

The awkward truth is that collective violence has been one way in which societies have reorganised themselves to become more humane and prosperous. But as societies changed, so did the reasons they went to war.

'People always want to know: what was the earliest war?' says bioarchaeologist Linda Fibiger of Edinburgh University. 'But it would be more interesting to ask: how did neolithic people define violence? What was their concept of war?'

Any debate over the decline – or not – of war must take into account its changing nature, Dwyer says, adding that it didn't stop changing 200 years ago. In the decades since the second world war, for example, major international conflicts have become less frequent, but small wars have proliferated. This has happened, argues Yale University historian Samuel Moyn in his new book, *Humane,* in part because over the 20th century the justification for war shifted to peacekeeping and the defence of human rights, ensuring that war shrank in scale but became 'for ever'.

The trouble with small-scale wars, as Clauset and others have found, is that they have a strong tendency to escalate, especially if they go on for a long time. In 2019, political scientist Bear Braumoeller of Ohio State University published *Only the Dead*, in which he argued that the risk of escalation today was as high as it had been when European leaders sent their troops to war in the summer of 1914, believing they would be home by Christmas.

'When it comes to the propensity of war to spiral out of control and produce mind-boggling death tolls, we live in the same world that they lived in,' he wrote.

Why war escalates so easily is not well understood, but Braumoeller says it's a 'good bet' that technology is a factor. Scientist Peter Turchin of the Complexity Science Hub in Vienna, one of Seshat's co-founders, agrees. He says that stepwise advances in military technology – he calls them 'military revolutions' – may have been major drivers of collective violence.

The military revolution, singular, is the term historians use to describe the period of rapid technological and social change that began in the 16th century with the advent of portable firearms. But Turchin says there were others. One of the most important got under way about 3,000 years ago, across a swath of Eurasia south of the steppes, when archers armed with iron-tipped arrows first mounted horses.

Each time, the technology handed an advantage to those who had it, stimulating a technological and eventually social arms race. And that technology wasn't even necessarily devised for military ends. The farming revolution, which ushered in the neolithic period, was also a military revolution, because the advances that gave farmers new tools also gave them new weapons. And some have argued that war became more lethal in the early 1800s in part because of the newfound ease of moving troops and supplies by rail.

'The upshot was that, with more soldiers on a given battlefield, it took more deaths on both sides to win a battle and therefore more deaths to win a war,' Braumoeller says.

Many people perceive technological change to be accelerating. The 20th century saw at least one military revolution, as a result of which we have nuclear weapons and the capacity to wage war in space. The early nuclear weapons were so destructive and so bad at hitting targets that they acted as effective deterrents and helped usher in this current period of stability, Morris says, but counterintuitively, we may have more grounds to worry now that they are generally smaller and more precise.

Morris sees parallels between the period we're living through now and the late 19th century, when international conflicts were few, but small-scale insurgencies and civil wars proliferated, and some of them, such as the Boer war, spiralled out of control. That long peace was finally shattered in 1914 and this one will be eventually too, he thinks.

What the cause and who the belligerent parties will be in the war that breaks the peace is not yet possible to say of course, though there has been much speculation – for example that it may involve Chinese military action against Taiwan. Nevertheless, for those who believe that the past can be instructive about the present, just not in the way Pinker does, *Better Angels* recalls a slew of books published on the eve of the first world war that proclaimed that war between the great powers was a thing of the past.

7 November 2021

Lessons from a war zone

Naked geopolitical ambition now trumps human rights.

By Aris Roussinos

To have been a war reporter over the past ten years is to have worked under the shadow of the modern American way of war. From Libya a decade ago to my last reporting trip in Syria in 2019, the outcome of the wars that followed the Arab Spring have been decided by the presence or absence of American air power.

I owe my life, no doubt, to an American pilot I've never met, who dropped a bomb a couple of years ago on ISIS fighters in the garden of the surrounded farmhouse in rural Deir Ezzor where I and SDF fighters huddled, waiting to be overrun. In these modern wars, the bombs that come hurtling out of the sky, rending the air like a bolt of lightning, land with pinpoint accuracy, transforming the course of a battle in an instant, like the judgment of an angry and invisible god.

Over the years, in battles across northeastern Syria, I watched the US Air Force rain down death on ISIS fighters, and then wandered, hours or days later, through the carnage that ensued: mangled bodies in their dozens, grey with cement dust or black with putrefaction, hurled by the explosion into all manner of strange and inhuman shapes.

In Raqqa five years ago, I embedded with Arab fighters of the SDF as they called in airstrikes against ISIS militants, which would level entire apartment blocks to dislodge one sniper. A year later, I followed local volunteers as they dragged the shrivelled, stinking bodies of airstrike victims from the city's rubble: ISIS wives or local civilians, identifiable only by

the detritus of a life suddenly cut short – passport photos, purses, makeup bags and soft toys.

The devastation of Raqqa after the battle, its apartment blocks crushed by the pinpoint precision of American military technology, looked hardly less total than that of rebel-held Eastern Aleppo, levelled by the wantonly imprecise barrel bombing of the Syrian regime, whose helicopters hovered unbearably over the city like flies over a dining table, disgorging their bombs at random. Yet even if the effect, in destroyed buildings, seemed much the same, surely the morality of the two approaches was different?

By emphasising precision and at least making a concerted effort to avoid civilian casualties, surely the American way of bombing is an act morally distinct from the indiscriminate punishment dealt out by the Syrian regime? If the intentions are good, can the results be evil?

It is, in part, to answer this question that the Yale legal scholar Samuel Moyn has written the new book *Humane*, an exploration of how the West's effort to conduct wars while minimising harm has had the unintended consequence of creating a world of forever war. He takes his cue from a speech Tolstoy puts into the mouth of his character Prince Andrei in *War and Peace*, in which the Russian aristocrat notes that war should be kept as brutal as possible, otherwise the temptation to keep waging it will become too great. As Moyn notes, 'humanitarianism led advocates to compromise

in pursuit of humane war and publics to feel good enough about themselves in the bargain to permit it to go on and on', with the result that 'endless war has become part of the way Americans live now'.

Rattling through the twin strands of the initially European effort to impose humanitarian rules on war, and the parallel American effort to abolish war altogether, Moyn assembles the evidence for his thesis: that from the Clinton era onwards, the mantra of Never Again has led the United States into an endless mission to bomb more and more of the earth in pursuit of global harmony. As he observes, 'of all the peoples in the annals of warfare, Americans are the ones who have invented a form of war righteously pursued as superior precisely for being more humane, and one tolerated by audiences for that very reason'.

A non-interventionist of a strain once dominant in American politics and only now slowly becoming the hegemonic worldview once again, Moyn is a critic of the process by which the postwar American empire legitimated itself through war for humanitarian ends. After World War Two, as he notes, 'self-styled internationalists... insisted that America had to commit to a globalised peace "scheme", yet 'it would only emerge slowly that this option meant committing the country to global war'.

Victory in World War Two and then in the Cold War both stood for Moyn as roads not taken, as American leaders refused to give up the prospect of global domination. Following the Vietnam War, as American military elites committed themselves to eliminating its indiscriminate bombing and targeted war crimes, the new discipline of International Humanitarian Law fused with the fact of America's sudden global preeminence to create the logic for liberal interventionism.

As Moyn notes, in the decades following Vietnam, the Western popular memory recentred the Holocaust into the war's retrospective justification: 'Peripheral in moral consciousness before, 'ethnic cleansing', culminating in genocide, became the defining evil of war past and present.' Coupled with unchallenged American hegemony, 'the new Holocaust memory coincided with the aftermath of decolonisation, and a skepticism along with it that others were up to the challenge of ruling themselves. The result was not a demand for peace but for interventionist justice.'

With the postwar taboo on initiating wars obscured, America was now morally entitled – encouraged, even – to launch its own wars in contravention of international law, as long as it could be argued that they prevented genocides: yet 'no-one asked at the time whether that implied that war itself – especially if it could be purged of its cruelty – was not that bad'. For Moyn as for Realist scholars, the two notionally distinct strands of interventionist thought, 'foreign policy neoconservatism and liberal internationalism', found themselves 'closer to each other than their followers liked to admit'.

From the Clinton era, which 'did the most to drive the drift into militarism, no matter the legality of the wars involved', through to the advice of scholars like John Yoo, who famously provided legal cover for the Bush administration's use of torture against captives in the War on Terror, Moyn traces the humanitarian and legal steps by which the American empire committed itself to endless, global war. Yet it was the Obama administration which really committed America to constant war, in a process by which the President elected on a peace platform became 'a permanent if humane war president', the architect of a massive expansion of drone strikes – a means to avoid the moral cloud of torture, by instead simply assassinating perceived wrongdoers – and of special forces operations on the ground.

Moyn's central thesis is that the well-intentioned humanisation of war functioned 'as a spoonful of sugar intended to help the medicine of endless war go down'; and that the push to forever war was driven by the liberal interventionist pressures of human rights activists, who demanded 'even more humane war than the good guys were willing to offer'. It is a neat argument, but surely an incomplete one.

It is primarily the vast disparity of power, and the almost total absence of risk to American pilots and drone operators that allows these wars to rumble on forever, not the minimising of harm to foreign civilians. It is only if American casualties were higher, and not civilian ones, that we would sooner see an end to America's wars of choice. The pinpoint accuracy with which a missile can be sent to its chosen target does not mean that, in the fog of war, the target was well chosen in the first place.

The recent extermination by drone of a blameless family in central Kabul only hit the headlines because it happened in the capital: if it had happened in the countryside, as has happened thousands of times in the past two decades, it is doubtful that anyone would know about it; and fundamentally, even in such a high profile case, few people in America cared much even then.

As for the push Moyn discerns by liberal interventionist commentators to drag American power into distant wars, a more cynical interpretation would be that moral causes only initiate American wars when the potential targets are already American foes. There was no clamour in Washington for a campaign against Saudi Arabia for its bombing of Yemen, for example, or against Bahrain for its lethal suppression of demonstrations, or against Turkey for its scorched earth suppression of armed revolts in the Kurdish east and invasions of northeastern Syria, or against Azerbaijan for its aggression against Armenia and beheading of captives. When the human rights oppressor is a US ally, advocates and journalists either tend not to make the case for intervention, or it is ignored.

Ultimately, for all his focus on the humanitisation of war, it is empire that Moyn is against: if America were militarily incapable of intervening in tangled squabbles at the other end of the world, it would feel no moral compulsion to do so. That compulsion may be the moral justification for empire, but fundamentally it is its product. Where there is no capacity to act, there is no moral compulsion. There will be no American war for the Uighurs, because it is not in America's power to launch or win one; human rights abuses like Xinjiang are deployed as a diplomatic tool to delegitimise China in the international sphere rather than as a call to arms.

Civilians will always die in wars, and Moyn does observe that it is better on the whole that fewer die, even if he is against wars in general, and American wars in particular. But did unipolarity foist on America the moral obligation to intervene in distant wars for humanitarian ends? Slightly unsatisfyingly, Moyn evades answering this question, but then it is perhaps an unresolvable one. He observes that the initial humanitarian cause in Libya morphed into 'an illegal regime change, with deplorable consequences for that country'. Yet the later intervention against ISIS improved the lives of many Syrian and Iraqi civilians, even if it extinguished the lives of many others.

But at this point, balancing this difficult central dilemma may already be a historical question. The 2015 Russian intervention in Syria marked the end of the unipolar moment by showing that a rival power, by committing itself to a cause peripheral to the United States's core concerns, can call the fading superpower's bluff. And contrary to Moyn's assertion that we may be entering an era of total US global policing, the rise of China has vastly accelerated the end of unchallenged unipolarity.

A war with China where the US may lose tens of thousands of personnel in the first day is a qualitatively different prospect from vaporising a defenceless presumed enemy at the push of a button, and the Biden administration does not seem in a hurry to enter into it. America's responsibility to protect was only ever a function of its capacity to do so. Now that capacity appears in doubt, the question is already moot.

We are back to a world of wars of necessity, for naked geopolitical advantage, and not wars of choice, driven by moral compulsion. The results, over the coming decades, may yet answer Moyn's unanswered question of whether America's attempted humanisation of war was really so bad after all.

2 December 2021

'I think there will be a war': Ukrainians wait for worst as eleventh-hour talks start

As diplomats meet in a desperate attempt to prevent conflict, people in Kiev tell world affairs editor Kim Sengupta how they fear it is too late, and that war is inevitable.

By Kim Sengupta

The last throws of the diplomatic dice are taking place in an increasingly desperate attempt to avoid a war in Europe amid grim warnings that Vladimir Putin will order an attack on Ukraine.

After days of talks with allies this week, Antony Blinken met Sergei Lavrov today in Geneva with flickering hopes of scaling back the confrontation, and avoiding a conflict that both sides accept will have devastating consequences.

The last meeting between the US secretary of state and the Russian foreign minister, in December, ended after just 40 minutes with exchanges of accusations and recriminations with demands that the Kremlin start pulling back the more than 100,000 troops massed on Ukraine's borders.

As they met, ordinary people in Ukraine continued to fear the worst, claiming that conflict was all but inevitable.

The threat of violent strife has grown significantly worse since December with more Russian forces moving into strategic positions needed for an offensive, and claims by the Americans that the Russians are planning 'false flag' operations as pretext for attacks.

They have also claimed that former Ukrainian government figures are being organised by the Kremlin to form a provisional government after invasion and occupation. On Thursday the US Treasury has imposed sanctions on two Ukrainian MPs and two former officials who are allegedly part of the plot.

The new talks take place in the wake of Joe Biden publicly declaring, to the surprise of those involved in the negotiations, that military action appeared to be inevitable. Vladimir Putin, he said, 'has to do something... My guess is he will move in'.

The US President went on to say that Nato was divided as it faces the crisis. 'It's one thing if it's a minor incursion, and then we end up having to fight about what to do and not do etc'. Ukraine's president, Volodymyr Zelensky, reposted 'there are no minor incursions. Just as there are no minor casualties and little grief from the loss of loved ones.'

Following meetings with British, French and German officials on Thursday, Mr Blinken said in Berlin that allowing an incursion into Ukraine by Russia would 'drag us all back to a much more dangerous and unstable time, when this continent, and this city, were divided in two... with the threat of all-out war hanging over everyone's heads'.

Speaking alongside Mr Blinken, Germany's new foreign minister, Annalena Baerbock, pledged immediate action against any Russian invasion and imposing measures that 'could have economic consequences for ourselves'. The country's new chancellor, Olaf Schulz, had stated earlier this week that Nord Stream 2, the pipeline project for Russian gas, may be halted if there is an attack on Ukraine.

Speaking in Australia, Liz Truss asked Vladimir Putin to 'desist and step back from Ukraine before he makes a massive strategic mistake'. Moscow, said the British foreign secretary, 'has not learned the lessons of history' and an 'invasion will only lead to a terrible quagmire and loss of life, as we know from the Soviet-Afghan war...'

It is, however, the Biden-led humiliating retreat by the west from Afghanistan that is seen by adversaries as well as some allies as heralding an era of 'western defeatism'.

A senior Ukrainian diplomat said : 'We saw what happened, and it is worrying. The Americans had invested 20 years in Afghanistan, they had quite a small force [about 2,400] and pulled out. Of course Afghanistan is far away, and what's happening here will affect Europe. We know the Russian plan is to try and do a deal directly with the Americans, cutting us out, and maybe the Europeans as well. We'll just have to see what happens.'

Ukrainian officials publicly insist that western support for their country has not wavered, and they point to the rise in military support from allies as proof of this.

Britain has become one of the most prominent suppliers, sending about 1,600 short-range NLAW (Next Generation Light Anti-Tank Weapon) missiles in a shuttle of RAF aircraft. There is also joint agreement for production of naval weaponry, including missile boats and minehunters, buttressed by a loan agreement of £1.7 billion from London.

The US has provided, in recent times, about $60 million (£45 million) worth of equipment, including additional Javelin anti-tank guided missiles to the ones already supplied. Washington has also signed a strategic defence framework with Kiev.

One of the most potent weapons in the Ukrainian armoury has not, however, come from the US or UK, but Recep Tayyip Erdogan. Turkey has sold TB2 drones to Kiev. The drones, which had been highly effective for Azerbaijan in its war against Moscow's ally, Armenia, have already been used, it is believed, by the Ukrainians in the Donbas, to destroy artillery of the separatist forces.

What the Ukrainians will not get from their allies are boots on the ground. As the British defence secretary, Ben Wallace, said in an interview while the missile deal was being set up: 'It's a fact it's not a member of Nato, so it is highly unlikely that anyone is going to send troops into Ukraine to challenge Russia... We shouldn't kid people on that we would.'

The west has also not sent the Ukrainians long-range offensive weaponry, knowing it will be viewed as highly provocative by Moscow. The Russians have the decisive advantage there with the deployment to the front of systems such as the BM-27 Uragan and the Iskander ballistic missiles which can hit Kiev from their positions. The joint military exercise with Belarus will see airpower augmented with the arrival of a Russian Su-35S fighter squadron.

The anti-tank missiles and the drones will be of use if there is close-quarter combat following a Russian invasion. Such urban fighting will be messy and bloody, but Petro Kravchuk can foresee that happening and also view it as a scenario which gives Ukraine some advantage.

Mr Kravchuk, a mechanical engineer, joined one of the volunteer battalions that fought in the Donbas and Lugansk in the last conflict and is now part of the country's reserves, and a member of the Civil Defence Force.

'I never thought it was over when I returned to Kiev after the last war and the Russian occupation. They had the Minsk agreement and all that, but there was always fighting, killing going on,' he told The Independent.

'We used anti-tank missiles in the anti-terrorist operation in the Donbas before. They were older models, but if we have newer Javelins and Stingers, yes it will make a difference. Of course they have a lot of firepower, but if they come into the cities it will be costly for them.

'I am not boasting about this. I do not want to see more fighting, more people getting killed. I was injured last time and that or worse may happen again. This should not be happening but it is the fault of the Russians, but also some of our own politicians.'

Mr Kravchuk, who was shot in the arm during the fight for Donetsk airport in 2014, continued : 'I have a wife, three children, I have parents, and brothers and sisters. I don't want to leave them to go and fight, but it looks like we may not have a choice. At the end we must defend our country.'

People in Ukraine have been living under the shadow of war for years and there had been a feeling among many that the worst predictions will not come to pass. But that appears to be changing, at least among some.

Galyna Nazarenko said that she had begun to feel very nervous for the first time since this the current standoff began. 'I think there will be a war, yes, unfortunately I think this will come,' she said. 'And I am not even sure that this time it will be just in the east.'

Spreading her hands towards Yaroslav Val Street in central Kiev, with people heading into shops and cafes in the snow, Ms Nazarenko said: 'We keep hearing that the Russians are putting more and more soldiers, tanks in that border area. We read that Putin wants to take Kiev and put in another government; there are all kinds of theories.'

Ms Nazarenko, a chemist, said she, her family and friends are being careful now about their travel plans.

'I have a brother working in Warsaw. I was going to visit him with my husband next week. But what happens if the fighting begins? The airport will probably get shut and we'll be away from our children,' she said. 'So we are postponing our trip to see what happens. But we don't think that things will get better; we think they will get pretty bad.'

Olena Tkachuk, a colleague of Ms Nazarenko, joined her for coffee as she was speaking.

'People in Europe cannot see how serious things are becoming. But it will affect other countries as well,' she said.

'But we must consider our own situation here. If the situation gets worse we may move to Lviv [in western Ukraine]; that may be safer. This is not the kind of conversation one should have in a normal society, but we are not living in normal times.'

21 January 2022

10 conflicts to watch in 2022

Troubling undercurrents in 2021 – from the U.S. to Afghanistan, Ethiopia or the climate emergency – didn't send battle deaths soaring or set the world ablaze. But as our look ahead to 2022 shows, many bad situations round the world could easily get worse.

After a year that saw an assault on the U.S. Capitol, horrific bloodshed in Ethiopia, a Taliban triumph in Afghanistan, great-power showdowns over Ukraine and Taiwan amid dwindling U.S. ambition on the global stage, COVID-19, and a climate emergency, it's easy to see a world careening off the tracks.

But maybe one could argue things are better than they seem.

After all, by some measures, war is in retreat. The number of people killed in fighting worldwide has mostly declined since 2014 – if you count only those dying directly in combat. According to the Uppsala Conflict Data Program, figures through the end of 2020 show battle deaths are down from seven years ago, mostly because Syria's terrible slaughter has largely subsided.

The number of major wars has also descended from a recent peak. Despite Russian President Vladimir Putin menacing Ukraine, states rarely go to war with one another. More local conflicts rage than ever, but they tend to be of lower intensity. For the most part, 21st-century wars are less lethal than their 20th-century predecessors.

A more cautious United States might also have an upside. The 1990s bloodletting in Bosnia, Rwanda, and Somalia; the post-9/11 Afghanistan and Iraq wars; Sri Lanka's murderous campaign against the Tamils; and the collapse of Libya and South Sudan all happened at a time of – and, in some cases, thanks to – a dominant U.S.-led West. That recent U.S. presidents have refrained from toppling enemies by force is a good thing. Besides, one shouldn't overstate Washington's sway even in its post-Cold War heyday; absent an invasion, it has always struggled to bend recalcitrant leaders (former Sudanese leader Omar al-Bashir, for example) to its will.

Still, if these are silver linings, they're awfully thin.

Battle deaths, after all, tell just a fraction of the story. Yemen's conflict kills more people, mostly women and young children, due to starvation or preventable disease than violence. Millions of Ethiopians suffer acute food insecurity because of the country's civil war. Fighting involving Islamists elsewhere in Africa often doesn't entail thousands of deaths but drives millions of people from their homes and causes humanitarian devastation.

Afghanistan's violence levels have sharply dropped since the Taliban seized power in August, but starvation, caused mostly by Western policies, could leave more Afghans dead – including millions of children – than past decades of fighting. Worldwide, the number of displaced people, most due to war, is at a record high. Battle deaths may be down, in other words, but suffering due to conflict is not.

Moreover, states compete fiercely even when they're not fighting directly. They do battle with cyber attacks, disinformation campaigns, election interference, economic coercion, and by instrumentalising migrants. Major and

regional powers vie for influence, often through local allies, in war zones. Proxy fighting has not so far sparked direct confrontation among meddling states. Indeed, some navigate the danger adeptly: Russia and Turkey maintain cordial relations despite backing competing sides in the Syrian and Libyan conflicts. Still, foreign involvement in conflicts creates the risk that local clashes light bigger fires.

Standoffs involving major powers look increasingly dangerous. Putin may gamble on another incursion into Ukraine. A China-U.S. clash over Taiwan is unlikely in 2022, but the Chinese and U.S. militaries increasingly bump up against each another around the island and in the South China Sea, with all the peril of entanglement that entails. If the Iran nuclear deal collapses, which now seems probable, the United States or Israel may attempt – possibly even early in 2022 – to knock out Iranian nuclear facilities, likely prompting Tehran to sprint toward weaponisation while lashing out across the region. One mishap or miscalculation, in other words, and interstate war could make a comeback.

And whatever one thinks of U.S. influence, its decline inevitably brings hazards, given that American might and alliances have structured global affairs for decades. No one should exaggerate the decay: U.S. forces are still deployed around the globe, NATO stands, and Washington's recent Asia diplomacy shows it can still marshal coalitions like no other power. But with much in flux, Washington's rivals are probing to see how far they can go.

Today's most dangerous flash points – whether Ukraine, Taiwan, or confrontations with Iran – relate in some way to the world struggling for a new equilibrium. Dysfunction in the United States hardly helps. A delicate transition of global power requires cool heads and predictability – not fraught elections and policy seesawing from one administration to the next.

As for COVID-19, the pandemic has exacerbated the world's worst humanitarian disasters and propelled the impoverishment, rising living costs, inequality, and joblessness that fuel popular anger. It had a hand this past year in a power grab in Tunisia, Sudan's coup, and protests in Colombia. The economic hurt COVID-19 is unleashing could strain some countries to a breaking point. Although it's a leap from discontent to protest, from protest to crisis, and from crisis to conflict, the pandemic's worst symptoms may yet lie ahead.

So while today's troubling undercurrents haven't yet set battle deaths soaring or the world ablaze, things still look bad. As this year's list shows all too starkly, they could easily get worse.

1. Ukraine

Whether Russia, which has been massing troops on the Ukrainian border, will again invade its neighbour remains unclear. But dismissing the menace as a bluff would be a mistake.

The Ukraine war began in 2014 when Putin, angered at what he saw as a Western-backed overthrow of a president friendly to Moscow, annexed Crimea and backed separatists in Ukraine's eastern Donbass region. Facing a military rout, Ukraine signed two peace accords, the Minsk agreements, largely on Russia's terms. Since then, separatists have held two breakaway areas in the Donbass.

What was for several years a simmering conflict heated up in 2021. A truce agreed to by Putin and Ukrainian President Volodymyr Zelensky, who came to power in 2019 promising to make peace, fell apart. In the spring of 2021, Putin amassed more than 100,000 troops near the border, only to withdraw many of them weeks later after a meeting with U.S. President Joe Biden. Since November, he's built up similar numbers.

Russia's grievances are clear enough. Moscow is upset at Ukraine's lack of follow-through with the Minsk agreements, particularly its denial of 'special status' to the breakaway regions – which entails autonomy and, as Moscow defines it, a say in foreign policy.

Putin, angry at what Moscow sees as decades of Western encroachment, has drawn a new red line on NATO, rejecting not only the idea that Ukraine would join the alliance, which (in reality) won't take place any time soon, but also growing military collaboration among Kyiv and NATO members, which is already happening. Russia proposes a new European order that would prevent NATO's further enlargement east and curb its military deployments and activities.

Russia may intend for the buildup to force concessions. But given Putin's track record and underestimation of the hostility Moscow inspires among Ukrainians outside separatist-held areas, no one should rule out another military adventure. If Russia plans to fight, its options vary from limited support of separatists to a full-scale assault.

Western powers, which too often have relied on bluster packaged as strategic ambiguity, need to clarify what they would do to support Ukraine, relay that to Moscow, and hold fast to red lines. Biden, who will meet Putin one-on-one in early January, has made a start by threatening damaging sanctions and a larger military buildup on NATO's eastern flank. Western leaders might also warn of reactions they don't intend but might struggle to control, perhaps including NATO members deploying more personnel to Ukraine itself, with all the attendant risks.

But deterrence will be short lived without efforts to de-escalate and lay the groundwork for more sustainable settlements in Ukraine and beyond. Choreographed de-escalation could involve Moscow pulling back forces, both sides limiting military exercises in the Black and Baltic Seas, a return to Minsk agreement negotiations, and talks on European security – even if the one-sided arrangement Russia proposes is out of the question.

In reality, no one will get what they want from the standoff. Kyiv may not like the Minsk agreements, but it signed them, and they remain the internationally accepted way out of the crisis. Putin hopes for a pliant neighbour in Ukraine, but that's a pipe dream – unless he's ready for a painful and costly occupation. Europe and the United States can neither deter without some risk of escalation nor resolve the Ukraine crisis without grappling with broader European security. As for Biden, he may want to focus on China but can't relegate Russia to the back burner.

2. Ethiopia

Two years ago, Ethiopia was a good news story. Ethiopian Prime Minister Abiy Ahmed appeared to be turning the page on decades of repressive rule. Instead, more than a year of fighting between Abiy's federal army and forces from the northern Tigray region has torn the country apart.

A small window may have just opened up to bring the war to a close.

Battlefield dynamics have fluctuated dramatically. Abiy first ordered federal troops into Tigray in November 2020 following a deadly attack on a military garrison there by loyalists of the region's ruling party, the Tigray People's Liberation Front (TPLF). Federal forces, supported by troops from enemy-turned-friend Eritrea, quickly advanced alongside forces from Ethiopia's Amhara region, which borders Tigray, installing an interim administration in the Tigrayan capital, Mekele, in December 2020.

Over subsequent months, TPLF leaders regrouped in the countryside, mobilizing Tigrayans livid at massacres, rapes, and havoc wreaked by federal and Eritrean troops. In a startling reversal, the rebels drove their enemies out of most of Tigray at the end of June before marching south. They then formed an alliance with an insurgent group in Ethiopia's populous, central Oromia region. An assault on the capital, Addis Ababa, appeared in the offing. Mid-November, however, brought another about-face. A counteroffensive by federal troops and allied militia forced Tigray forces to withdraw back to their home region.

But if federal forces, for now, are ascendant, both sides command strong support and could drum up more recruits. Neither is likely to deliver a mortal blow.

Brutal fighting has embittered an already acrimonious dispute. Abiy casts the war as a battle for the Ethiopian state's survival. Many Ethiopians outside Tigray revile the TPLF, which dominated a repressive regime that ruled Ethiopia for decades before Abiy's election.

Abiy paints TPLF leaders as power-hungry spoilers, bent on trashing his modernized vision for the country. In contrast, Tigrayan leaders said their initial attack that triggered the war preempted a campaign to subjugate Tigray by Abiy and the TPLF's old foe, Eritrean President Isaias Afwerki, with whom Abiy signed a 2018 peace deal. They see Abiy's reforms as an attempt to water down Ethiopian regions' rights to self-rule.

More war would spell more disaster. Fighting has already killed tens of thousands of people and uprooted millions of Ethiopians from their homes. All sides stand accused of atrocities. Much of Tigray, denied aid by federal authorities, is nearing famine. The wounds the bloodletting has left on Ethiopia's social fabric will be hard to heal. Neighbours beyond Eritrea could get pulled in. Sudan, another good news story that turned sour in 2021 when its generals grabbed power, has its own disputes with Ethiopia over territory in the fertile borderlands of al-Fashqa and the Grand Ethiopian Renaissance Dam on the Nile, where Addis Ababa has started to fill the reservoir. With Ethiopia in turmoil, Sudan – along with Egypt – could see a moment to press its advantage.

Recent battlefield developments may have opened a small window. Tigrayan leaders have dropped a key condition for talks, namely that Amhara forces leave disputed areas they seized in western Tigray. In late December, federal authorities announced they would not advance further to try and vanquish Tigrayan forces. Diplomats should now push for a truce to get humanitarian aid into Tigray and explore whether compromise might be feasible. Without that, bloodshed and hunger will continue, with terrible consequences for Ethiopians and, potentially, the region.

3. Afghanistan

If 2021 brought one chapter of Afghanistan's decades long tragedy to a close, another is starting. Since the Taliban's seizure of power in August, a humanitarian catastrophe has loomed. U.N. data suggests millions of Afghan children could starve. Western leaders shoulder much of the blame.

The Taliban's win was swift but long in the making. For years, and especially since early 2020, when Washington signed a deal with the Taliban pledging to withdraw U.S. forces, insurgents advanced through the countryside, encircling provincial and district centres. In the Spring and Summer of 2021, they began seizing towns and cities, often persuading Afghan army commanders demoralized by the impending end of Western support to surrender. The government collapsed in mid-August, and the Taliban entered Kabul mostly without a fight. It was a stunning end to a political order Western powers had spent two decades helping to build.

The world responded to the Taliban's takeover by freezing Afghan state assets, halting budgetary aid, and offering only limited sanctions relief for humanitarian purposes. (The Taliban are sanctioned by the United Nations and Western governments.)

The new government can't pay civil servants. The economy has tanked. The financial sector is paralysed. All this comes on top of a punishing drought. Although overall violence levels are significantly down from a year ago, the Taliban face a vicious fight against the Islamic State's local branch.

The new regime has done little to endear itself to donors. Its interim cabinet includes almost exclusively Taliban figures, no women, and mostly ethnic Pashtuns. Early Taliban decisions, notably closing girls' schools in many provinces, sparked international outrage (some have since reopened). Reports have emerged of extra-judicial killings of former soldiers and police.

Still, Western decision-makers bear the lion's share of responsibility for Afghans' plight. The sudden cutoff of funds to an entirely aid-dependent state has been devastating. The United Nations estimates 23 million people, more than half the population, will suffer from hunger this winter. Humanitarian support alone can't stave off disaster. Donors are squandering genuine gains their funds helped deliver over the past two decades, notably in health and education.

There is another way. International financial institutions, having released a small part of the almost $2 billion earmarked for Afghanistan, should disperse the rest. The United Nations and United States, which have now lifted some sanctions to allow in humanitarian aid, should go further by easing restrictions to permit regular economic activity. Biden should release Afghanistan's frozen assets, with an initial tranche to test the waters.

If the White House, loath to underwrite Taliban rule, won't take that step, internationally supervised currency swaps could infuse dollars into the economy. Propping up health care, the education system, food provision, and other basic services should be priorities – even if this requires Western policymakers to work through Taliban ministries.

The alternative is to let Afghans die, including millions of children. Of all the blunders the West has made in Afghanistan, this one would leave the ugliest stain.

4. The United States and China

Shortly after pulling out of Afghanistan, the United States announced a new pact with Australia and the United Kingdom to counter China. Known as AUKUS, the deal will help Canberra acquire nuclear-powered submarines. It was a stark illustration of Washington's aspirations to move from combating Islamist militants to major power politics and deterring Beijing.

In Washington, one of the few views shared across the aisle is that China is an adversary the United States is inexorably at loggerheads with. U.S. leaders see past decades of engaging China as enabling the rise of a rival that exploits international bodies and rules to its own ends, repressing opposition in Hong Kong, behaving atrociously in Xinjiang, and bullying its Asian neighbours. Competition with China is becoming an ordering principle of U.S. policy.

Biden's China strategy, while not precisely articulated, entails keeping the United States the dominant power in the Indo-Pacific, where Beijing's military capacity has ballooned. Biden appears to see the costs of Chinese regional primacy as graver than the risk of confrontation. Concretely, that meant shoring up U.S. alliances and partnerships in Asia as well as elevating the importance of Taiwan's security to U.S. interests. Top officials also make stronger statements backing Southeast Asian countries' maritime claims in the South China Sea.

Beijing sees things differently. Chinese leaders, having hoped at first for improved ties with Washington under Biden, now worry more about him than they did about former U.S. President Donald Trump, a leader they hoped was an anomaly. They express disappointment at Biden's decision not to roll back trade tariffs or sanctions as well as his efforts to mobilize other countries. They recoil at rhetoric about democracy and human rights, which they view as ideological bombast that implicitly calls their government's legitimacy into question.

In essence, Beijing wants a sphere of influence in which its neighbours are sovereign but deferential. It views dominance of the first island chain – which stretches from the Kuril Islands, past Taiwan, and into the South China Sea – as vital to its growth, security, and ambition to be a world naval power.

Over the past year, while not disavowing its official 'peaceful reunification' policy, Beijing escalated military activity near Taiwan, flying record numbers of jets and bombers as well as conducting drills near the island. Beijing's growing military clout and assertiveness have provoked more dire assessments in Washington about the threat of a Chinese assault on Taiwan.

A virtual meeting in November between Biden and Chinese President Xi Jinping took some of the edge off the frosty rhetoric of previous months. It could yield more working-level engagement, including the resumption of defence dialogues. In 2022, with the Beijing Winter Olympics, the 20th Party Congress, and U.S. midterm congressional elections, both sides likely want quiet fronts abroad, even if they rattle sabers for audiences at home. The nightmare scenario – a Chinese attempt to seize Taiwan, potentially forcing the United States to come to Taipei's defence – is unlikely for now.

Still, the two giants' rivalry casts a long shadow over world affairs and heightens dangers across flash points in East Asia. Beijing sees scant benefits in cooperating on issues like climate change when Washington frames the relationship as competitive. Along the first island chain, things are particularly frightening. Warplanes flying close to one another near Taiwan, for example, ort warships crossing paths in the South China Sea are more common. A mishap would ratchet up tensions.

When U.S. and Chinese planes collided in 2001 during a period of reasonable calm between Beijing and Washington, it took months of intense diplomacy to resolve the spat. Today, it would be harder – and the danger of escalation greater.

5. Iran vs. the United States and Israel

The nail-biting brinkmanship between Tehran and Washington instigated under Trump may be over. But as hope of reviving the Iran nuclear deal fades, another escalation looms.

Biden took office pledging to rejoin the nuclear deal. His predecessor had unilaterally withdrawn Washington in 2018, reimposing sanctions on Iran – which, in turn, stepped up its nuclear development and power projection across the Middle East. The Biden administration lost time posturing about who should make the first move and refusing substantive goodwill gestures. Still, for a few months, talks made some progress.

Then, in June, Ebrahim Raisi won Iran's presidential election, giving hard-liners control of all the Islamic Republic's key power centres. After a five-month hiatus, Iran returned to the table, driving a harder bargain. At the same time, it is accelerating nuclear development. When the deal took effect six years ago, Iran's breakout time – the time it would take to enrich enough fissile material for a nuclear weapon – was around 12 months. It's now estimated at three to six weeks and shrinking.

Although Tehran hasn't unilaterally pulled out of the deal like Trump did, it's still playing with fire. Failure to restore the deal in the months ahead would likely make the original agreement moot, given Iran's technological advances. There are options: Diplomats could pursue a more comprehensive deal, though that would be a hard slog given the bad blood the original deal's demise would entail, or they could seek an interim 'less-for-less' arrangement that caps Iran's continued nuclear progress for limited sanctions relief. But a collapse of negotiations is a real possibility.

That would be a disaster. Iran's nuclear program would continue unhindered. For Washington, accepting Iran as a threshold nuclear state – one able to build a bomb even if not yet having done so – will likely prove to be too bitter a pill to swallow. The alternative would be to approve or join Israeli strikes aimed at setting back Tehran's nuclear capability.

If that happened, Iran's leaders – whose calculations are likely informed by the toppling of former Libyan leader Muammar al-Qaddafi, who forfeited his nuclear weapons program, and the respect Trump showed toward nuclear-armed North Korea – may well sprint toward weaponisation.

Tehran would also likely lash out across the Middle East. Nascent efforts at de-escalation between Iran and Persian Gulf monarchies may help lower risks, but Iraq, Lebanon, and Syria would all be in the crossfire. Incidents could heighten the danger of direct confrontation between Iran and the United States, Israel, or the two allies together, which the parties have thus far avoided despite provocations. Such clashes could easily spin out of control on the ground, at sea, in cyberspace, or through covert operations.

Talks fizzling could, in other words, combine all the dangers from the period before the 2015 deal with the worst worries of the Trump years.

6. Yemen

Yemen's war faded from headlines in 2021 but remains devastating and could be poised to get worse.

Houthi rebels have encircled and advanced into the oil- and gas-rich governorate of Marib. Long underrated as a military force, the rebels appear to be running an agile and evolving multifront campaign, pairing offensives with outreach to soften local tribal leaders' resistance. They now control Al-Bayda, a governorate neighbouring Marib, and have made inroads into Shabwa, farther east, thus cutting off supply lines to Marib. Of Marib governorate itself, only the main city and hydrocarbon facilities nearby remain in the hands of President Abed Rabbo Mansour Hadi's internationally recognized government.

Should those sites fall, it would mark a sea change in the war. The Houthis would score an economic as well as a military victory. With Marib's oil and gas, the Houthis will be able to bring down fuel and electricity prices in areas under their control, thus bolstering their image as a governing authority deserving of international legitimacy. The loss of Marib, the Hadi government's last bastion in the north, would likely herald the president's political demise.

Some nominally Hadi-aligned Yemenis already mutter about replacing him with a presidential council. That would further undercut the government's international status, likely reinforcing the Houthis' resistance to peace talks.

Anyone hoping that a Houthi win would presage the war's end is banking on an illusion. In southern Yemen, anti-Houthi factions outside Hadi's coalition – namely southern separatists backed by the United Arab Emirates and a faction led by Tareq Saleh, nephew of Yemen's late long-serving leader – would battle on. The Houthis, who see the war as pitting their nationalist forces against neighbouring Saudi Arabia – which backs Hadi with air power – would likely continue cross-border attacks.

The United Nations' new envoy for Yemen, Hans Grundberg, who assumed his role at the helm of international peacemaking efforts last September, needs to do two things at once. First, he should seek to avert a battle for Marib city by hearing out, without necessarily accepting, Houthi proposals and pushing for a government counteroffer that reflects the reality of today's power balance. The U.N. also needs a new peacemaking approach that goes beyond two-party talks between the Houthis, on the one hand, and the Hadi government and its Saudi backers, on the other. Yemen's war is a multiparty conflict, not a binary power struggle; any hope of reaching a genuine settlement requires more seats at the table.

7. Israel-Palestine

This past year saw the fourth and most destructive Gaza-Israel war in just over a decade, illustrating again that the peace process is dead and a two-state solution looks less likely than ever.

The trigger for this latest outbreak was occupied East Jerusalem. The threatened eviction of Palestinian residents of the Sheikh Jarrah neighbourhood coincided in April 2021 with clashes during Ramadan between stone-throwing youth and Israeli police using lethal force on the compound that comprises the Haram al-Sharif, holy to Muslims, and the Temple Mount, holy to Jews.

That set off a chain reaction. Hamas, which controls Gaza, fired long-distance rockets indiscriminately into Israel. Israel responded with a harsh aerial assault, sparking an 11- day conflict that killed more than 250 people, almost all Palestinians, and left in ruins what remained of Gaza's civilian infrastructure. West Bank Palestinians demonstrating in solidarity were met with the Israeli army's live fire. In Israeli cities, Palestinian citizens took to the streets, sometimes clashing with West Bank settlers and other right-wing Jews, often supported by Israeli police.

While hostilities were all too familiar, this bout brought new elements. Palestinians, for the first time in decades, transcended their fragmentation by joining voices across the West Bank, East Jerusalem, Gaza, and Israel itself. Also striking was debate in Western capitals, Washington especially. Democrats, including mainstream figures, used unusually stern language about Israel's bombardment, suggesting that, among the party, views of the conflict are evolving.

Still, fundamentals remain unchanged. Though Israelis were apparently taken aback by the intensity of Hamas's rocket fire, the war provoked no rethink of Israel's Gaza policy – economic strangulation to weaken Hamas and divide Palestinians; 'mowing the grass' every few years to stifle attacks – or its general treatment of Palestinians. Abroad, most capitals wrung their hands but did little. The Biden administration, despite Democrats' new tone, claimed to conduct 'quiet, intensive diplomacy' but more or less allowed the conflict to run its course.

Nor have the months since brought hope. A hodgepodge coalition ousted Israel's longest-serving prime minister, Benjamin Netanyahu, in June. After Netanyahu's belligerence, the new government put a softer face on Israel's foreign relations and declared its hope to 'shrink' the conflict by improving the occupied territories' economies and marginally strengthening the Palestinian Authority, which partly rules the West Bank. Yet it continues to expand illegal settlements and repress Palestinians much as its predecessors did. In October, it outlawed six respected Palestinian civil society groups on specious terrorism charges.

For anyone still eager to renew negotiations, the last year was cause for despair. The centre of gravity in Israeli politics has long since shifted away from peace, as successive governments have abandoned talks in all but name. Most Palestinians have lost faith they will win statehood through negotiations.

There are ways to buy quiet: a longer-term truce and opening up of Gaza; ending expulsions of Palestinians in East Jerusalem; returning to preexisting arrangements that kept the holy sites reasonably calm.

But those can only stave off the next war for so long. Diplomats' lip service to a two-state solution that is all but out of reach gives cover for Israel to advance de facto annexation of the West Bank. Better now would be to try to end Israeli impunity for violations of Palestinian rights. It's time, in other words, to address the situation on the ground as it is.

8. Haiti

The Caribbean nation has long been tormented by political crises, gang warfare, and natural disasters. Nevertheless, this past year stands out for many Haitians as particularly bleak. Few expect a brighter 2022.

In July, hit men assassinated President Jovenel Moïse in his home; his security detail apparently did nothing about it. Shellshocked elites squabbled over who would run the country. (Succession lines were muddled as Moïse had appointed Ariel Henry as his new prime minister but Henry had not yet been sworn in.) Henry eventually became the country's interim leader but has struggled to assert authority.

An earthquake in August destroyed much of southern Haiti. Rampant kidnappings by gangs that lord over much of the capital of Port-au-Prince have hampered international relief efforts. Criminals' seizure of oil terminals brought the country to a standstill in early November. Haiti, meanwhile, lags behind the rest of the Americas in distributing COVID- 19 vaccines. Increasing numbers of Haitians are seeking better prospects abroad; many new departures – and indeed many Haitians who left the island some time ago – are camped out along the southern U.S. border.

As for the post-Moïse transition, two factions propose competing plans. Henry and several parties have inked a deal allowing him to rule until elections in 2022. In contrast, the Commission for a Haitian Solution to the Crisis, an umbrella group of civil society organizations and political parties, insists the country's wounds cut so deep that only root-and-branch reform can stanch the bleeding. They want a two-year transition, with a council more representative of society holding power until new polls. With the constitution largely a dead letter (postponed elections mean two-thirds of Senate seats are empty) and responsibility for Moïse's killing unclear, Haiti's immediate stability requires reconciling these two options.

Gangs also have political clout. Jimmy 'Barbecue' Chérizier, a former police officer who is capo of the so-called G9 criminal alliance that seized the oil terminals, has demanded that Henry resign. Police corruption, an enfeebled judicial system, and the hemisphere's highest poverty rates provide ideal conditions for gangs to recruit and expand. Chérizier himself combines brute force with politicking designed to appeal to impoverished, unemployed young men.

Many Haitians bristle at the idea of a new U.N. peacekeeping mission, let alone U.S. military intervention, but without some overseas help it is hard to see Haiti escaping its predicament. Donors supporting a specialized joint Haitian-U.N. office tasked with prosecuting top officials, police, and judges accused of serious crimes could help reduce violence and sever ties between criminals and politicians.

The first priority, though, is for Haitians to agree on a new transition plan. Without it, they will face another year of gridlock, crime, and unrest as more depart in search of better lives elsewhere.

9. Myanmar

Since the February 2021 coup, a crackdown by the country's military (known as the Tatmadaw) on mostly peaceful protests has fuelled broad-based resistance, ranging from civil disobedience to armed clashes with security forces. A deadly stalemate exacts a terrible human toll.

If the generals hoped to reboot Myanmar's politics, they miscalculated. Piqued at Aung San Suu Kyi and her National League for Democracy's landslide win in the November 2020 elections, military leaders called the vote rigged and detained civilian politicians. Their plans for new elections seemingly aimed to install friendlier faces to power. Instead, mass protests against military involvement in politics rocked towns and cities. A crackdown resulting in hundreds of deaths fuelled fiercer resistance.

Since then, deposed lawmakers set up their own National Unity Government (NUG) and in September called for revolt against the regime. While the NUG is still developing its own military capability, resistance forces, many of which support the NUG but are mostly not under its direct control, stage attacks daily, ambushing military convoys, bombing regime-linked targets, and assassinating local officials, suspected informants, and others they see as junta loyalists.

Myanmar's ethnic armed groups, some of which comprise tens of thousands of fighters and control vast upland areas, have themselves adapted. Some have remained aloof; others, responding to constituents' anger at the coup, have resumed fighting the Tatmadaw. Some shelter dissidents, provide them military training, and are negotiating with the NUG. For its part, the NUG has sought to win over armed groups, including by promising a federal system for Myanmar.

Majority views about ethnic minorities are also changing: Long blamed for Myanmar's problems, minorities' demands for a fairer share of power today enjoy more support. While a united front against the regime is unlikely, given rebels' historical rivalries, significant political and military cooperation is taking place.

For its part, the Tatmadaw has doubled down. It detains, sometimes executes, and routinely tortures opponents, often abducting kin as hostages. Battalions have crushed urban dissent, using tactics that aim to kill as many people as possible. (A U.N.-backed investigation's preliminary analysis suggests crimes against humanity.)

In rural areas, the army fights new resistance groups with old counterinsurgency methods, namely its 'four cuts' strategy, aimed at denying rebels food, funds, intelligence, and recruits. It targets civilians; in the latest of many reported incidents, credible accounts suggest that at the end of December the military massacred dozens of civilians fleeing violence in eastern Myanmar. The regime has also attempted to persuade armed groups from entering formal alliances with the NUG, in some cases keeping groups – including the Arakan Army, with which it fought a brutal war in 2019-2020 – off the battlefield.

Having locked up their rivals – Aung San Suu Kyi has already been sentenced to two years' imprisonment and could end up locked up for life – the generals are moving to amend electoral rules in their favour and hold a vote in 2023. However, any poll that would usher in a military-backed government would be seen as a farce.

The standoff's human cost is devastating. Myanmar's

economy is free-falling, the national currency has crashed, health and education systems have crumbled, poverty rates are estimated to have doubled since 2019, and half of all households cannot afford enough food. Myanmar's generals, convinced of their role at the country's helm, are steering it off a cliff.

For the most part, the world is losing interest. While outside actors have little influence on the Tatmadaw, it is critical that they keep trying to get aid in without empowering the regime. They can also usefully throw greater weight behind the diplomatic efforts of the Association of Southeast Asian Nations, which have so far been mostly dysfunctional, and the new U.N. special envoy. Beyond the human toll, a collapsed state in the heart of the strategically vital Indo-Pacific region serves no one's interests.

10. Islamist militancy in Africa

Since 2017, when the Islamic State lost its so-called caliphate in the Middle East, Africa has suffered some of the world's most ferocious battles between states and jihadis. Islamist militancy on the continent is nothing new, but revolts linked to the Islamic State and al Qaeda have surged in recent years.

Weak states struggle against nimble militant factions across vast hinterlands where central governments hold little sway. Parts of the Sahel have seen spiralling bloodshed, mostly due to fighting involving jihadis, whose reach has extended from northern Mali to the country's centre, into Niger, and across rural Burkina Faso.

Boko Haram's insurgency has lost the swaths of northeastern Nigeria it controlled some years ago, and the movement has fractured. But splinter groups still wreak tremendous harm around Lake Chad. In East Africa, al-Shabab, the continent's oldest-surviving Islamist rebellion, remains a potent force, despite more than 15 years of efforts to defeat it. The group holds large parts of Somalia's rural south, operates shadow courts and extorts taxes beyond those areas, and occasionally mounts attacks in neighbouring countries.

Africa's newest jihadi fronts – in northern Mozambique and eastern Democratic Republic of the Congo – are also troubling. Insurgents who claim a new Islamic State province in Mozambique's Cabo Delgado region have stepped up attacks on security forces and civilians. Nearly a million people have fled the fighting. Militants have loose ties to Islamic State networks that stretch both up the continent's east coast and into Congo's war-torn east. There, another Islamist rebel group – a faction of the Allied Democratic Forces, a Ugandan militia that has long operated in Congo – now declares itself an Islamic State affiliate. It launched attacks in the Ugandan capital of Kampala last November.

Mozambique's government, which long resisted outside involvement in Cabo Delgado, finally agreed last year to let in Rwandan troops and units from the Southern African Development Community (SADC), a regional bloc. Those forces have reversed insurgent gains, though militants appear to be regrouping. Rwandan and SADC forces risk a protracted war.

In Somalia and the Sahel, Western impatience could be decisive. Foreign forces – the EU-funded African Union Mission in Somalia, or AMISOM, and French and other European forces in the Sahel – help keep jihadis at bay. Yet military operations often alienate locals and further erode relations between them and state authorities.

There's little to show for years of foreign efforts to build up indigenous armies. Malian colonels have seized power in Bamako twice in the space of just over a year, while the regional G5 Sahel force, comprising troops from Mali and its neighbours, also struggles against jihadis. (Chad recently pulled out some of its troops from the force, fearing upheaval at home.) As for the Somali security forces, units, caught up in political bickering, often shoot at each other.

If foreign efforts wind down, battlefield dynamics would undoubtedly shift, perhaps decisively, in the militants' favour. In Somalia, al-Shabab could seize power in Mogadishu much as the Taliban did in Kabul. Intervening foreign powers are caught as they were in Afghanistan: unable to achieve their goals but fearful of what will follow if they exit. For now, they appear set to stay.

Even so, a rethink in both places – entailing a greater civilian role alongside military campaigns – is overdue. The Sahel governments need to improve their relations with citizens in the countryside. Somalia needs to repair relations among elites; late December saw another eruption in a drawn-out election feud. More controversial is talking to jihadis. It won't be easy: Somalia's neighbours, which contribute troops to AMISOM, oppose any engagement; and while Sahel governments have been more open, France rejects negotiations. No one knows whether compromise with militants is feasible, what it would entail, or how populations would view it.

But the military-centric approach has mostly spawned more violence. If foreign powers don't want the same dilemma haunting them in a decade's time, they need to prepare the ground for talks with militant leaders.

29 December 2021

Originally published in *Foreign Policy: 10 Conflicts to Watch in 2022*.

War devastates the lives of children: what the research tells us, and what can be done

An article from *The Conversation*.

THE CONVERSATION

By Roos van der Haer, Assistant Professor of International Relations at the Institute of Political Science, Leiden University

Amnesty International published a report recently on the situation in Niger that highlighted the devastating consequences of war for children. In Niger's Tillabéri region, hundreds of people have died or fled their homes, and food reserves and livestock have been attacked. Armed groups in this region, such as the Islamic State in the Greater Sahara and the al-Qaida-affiliated Jama'at Nusrat al-Islam wal-Muslimin, are increasingly targeting children.

As the report states, many Nigerian children have been killed, deprived of the opportunity to go to school, or forcibly displaced. Young boys are increasingly recruited to be soldiers, while girls in some areas of the region have faced restrictions on their ability to leave the home and, at times, have been forced to marry fighters. According to Amnesty International, Niger is at a precipice: an entire generation of children is growing up surrounded by death and destruction.

Niger is not unique in this sense. In many conflict areas, children are especially susceptible to the effects of war. In 2019, researchers at the Peace Research Institute in Oslo estimated that almost two thirds of the world's children were living in a conflict-ridden country. They also estimated that more than 415 million children – over one in six – were living less than 50km from where the actual fighting took place.

The impact on children

Psychologists have emphasised that the exposure to war during childhood and adolescence can pose serious mental health risks and can negatively influence a child's development. They have frequently demonstrated that children involved in war often experience symptoms of trauma and distress; they have nightmares, have problems concentrating, are extremely fearful or experience high levels of anxiety.

Repeated exposure to warfare during development can even cause post-traumatic stress disorder, depression, and severe personality changes. Post-traumatic stress disorder is often associated with negative behaviour against their own family, the expression of anger and hostility to others, addiction, and self-harm.

The severity of these potential mental health issues depend on many factors, such as the type of violence a child is exposed to or how often they have experienced potential traumatic events.

Economists, sociologists, and other social scientists have emphasised that growing up in a conflict affected area can also indirectly harm children. For example, war often disrupts and destroys children's education. Schools are attacked, teachers disappear, and children are often prevented from attending school out of fear of recruitment or violence.

Research has highlighted the adverse impact of conflict exposure in terms of reducing the numbers of years spend in school. These effects have been shown in turn to impact considerably future life prospects of affected children: children exposed to war experience greater reading problems, have less access to the labour market, are less likely to find high-skilled jobs, and will earn significantly less than those children that were not exposed to the war.

My own research has shown that the recruitment of children can also negatively influence the stability of the country in the short and long run. First, the recruitment of children by rebel groups makes a conflict last longer. With the recruitment of children, rebel groups can increase their size and power, which ultimately results in the conflict being prolonged. Second, conflicts in which children are recruited are more likely to recur in later periods of time.

Given these negative consequences, it is not a surprise that Amnesty International has called for urgent action by the Nigerian government and its international partners.

What can be done

Research has shown the added value of humanitarian assistance in protecting children during and after conflict. One can think about setting up psycho-social programmes, that help children and their families to recover from the conflict's psychological burden.

Children's well-being also profits from the creation of safe areas in which they can participate in activities, socialise, learn, and play. For instance, schools need to be protected and supported during and after conflict. If schools are closed due to attacks or threats, alternative ways of providing education to these children need to be implemented. This does not only create some normalcy in the lives of the very young, but schools might also protect children from recruitment and help their recovery once they come out of the armed groups.

Evidence also suggests that sustained attention must be given to community efforts. Communities can not only protect children but also impact the healing process. Due to the current volatile situation, however, the availability and implementation of this type of support is very limited in Niger. Unless the Nigerian authorities and international partners address how the war has targeted children, they risk creating a lost generation of children that might negatively impact the short and long-term stability of the country.

28 September 2021

Attacks on children in war zones almost triple since 2010

Some 45 violations – including killings, maiming and sexual violence – carried out against youngsters every single day over last 10 years.

By Colin Drury

Attacks on children forced to live in conflict zones have almost tripled over the last decade, the United Nations has said.

Some 170,000 violations against youngsters – including killing, maiming, sexual violence and child recruitment – have been verified since 2010, Unicef reports.

The figure amounts to the equivalent of 45 abuses every single day for 10 years.

But even that may be just the tip of the iceberg, it is said: many thousands more attacks are thought to have gone unreported.

'Conflicts around the world are lasting longer, causing more bloodshed and claiming more young lives,' Henrietta Fore, executive director of Unicef, said. 'Attacks on children continue unabated as warring parties flout one of the most basic rules of war: the protection of children.'

In 2018, the last year for which full figures are available, the UN verified more than 24,000 violations – almost three times higher than the corresponding figure collated in 2010. Children in Syria, Yemen and Afghanistan have been particularly at risk, Ms Fore added. But despicable attacks have also happened in Nigeria, where teenagers were used as suicide bombers, and in Myanmar where Muslim children in Rakhine State were reported to have been killed by government soldiers.

Airstrikes against schools and the use of youngsters as human shields have also added to the tally.

The shock figure comes as new analysis also revealed an estimated 6.9 million children across Europe and Asia are currently facing winter in temporary shelters, having been displaced by war.

That includes 2.5 million youngsters who have fled Syria and 300,000 who have left homes in eastern Ukraine, says Save The Children, which compiled the figure.

The charity identified 12 countries struggling with high numbers of these displaced youngsters where temperatures regularly hit freezing at this time of year.

Many such children, it said, are facing a fight for survival as they live in camps, squat in disused buildings or are housed in bare containers.

Rachael Cummings, director of humanitarian public health at the organisation, said: 'Millions have escaped vicious conflict or turmoil in search of safety. Yet for some the bitter winter could be as dangerous as the threats they left behind. 'Last winter in a matter of weeks freezing temperatures and harsh conditions in Syria killed 15 children who had fled conflict. Sometimes canvas or plastic sheeting just millimetres thick, or crumbling walls of abandoned buildings, are all that separate shivering, exhausted children from the elements as temperatures plummet.'

30 December 2019

Six grave violations against children in times of war

How children have become frontline targets in armed conflicts.

From widespread killing, maiming, abduction and sexual violence to recruitment into armed groups and strikes on schools and hospitals, as well as essential water facilities – children living in conflict zones around the world continue to come under attack on a shocking scale.

To better monitor, prevent, and end these attacks, the United Nations Security Council has identified and condemned six grave violations against children in times of war: Killing and maiming of children; recruitment or use of children in armed forces and armed groups; attacks on schools or hospitals; rape or other grave sexual violence; abduction of children; and denial of humanitarian access for children.

To mark the 25th anniversary of Graça Machel's report on the impact of armed conflict on children, UNICEF has released a statement with the Secretary General's Special Representative for Children and Armed Conflict calling for urgent action to protect children in war.

Armed forces and armed groups are required by international humanitarian law to take measures to protect civilians, including children, who are particularly vulnerable during times of war.

1. Killing and maiming of children

Killing and maiming of children can be a result of direct targeting or indirect actions, including torture. Killing and maiming can occur through crossfire, landmines, cluster munitions, improvised or other indiscriminate explosive devices or even in the context of military operations, house demolitions, search-and-arrest campaigns, or suicide attacks.

For example, the use of explosive weapons – particularly in populated areas – continues to have a devastating impact on children. In 2020 alone, explosive weapons and explosive remnants of war were responsible for at least 47 per cent of all child casualties. Between 2005 and 2020, more than 104,100 children were verified as killed or maimed in situations of armed conflict, with more than two-thirds of these verified since 2014.

2. Recruitment or use of children in armed forces and armed groups

Recruitment or use of children in armed forces and armed groups refers to compulsory, forced, or voluntary conscription or enlistment of children into any kind of armed force or armed group. Children continue to be recruited and used by parties to conflict at alarming rates. The use of boys and girls by armed forces or armed groups can be in any capacity, including as fighters, cooks, porters, messengers and spies, or when they are subjected to sexual exploitation.

Between 2005 and 2020, more than 93,000 children were verified as recruited and used by parties to conflict, although the actual number of cases is believed to be much higher.

The UN Country Task Forces on Monitoring and Reporting, or their equivalent, verified the recruitment and use of at least 1,000 children in at least 15 different countries over this period.

3. Attacks on schools or hospitals

Attacks on schools or hospitals include the targeting of schools or medical facilities that cause the total or partial destruction of such facilities. Schools and hospitals should be protected spaces, where children are safe even in times of conflict, yet continued attacks on such facilities have underscored the catastrophic impact of armed conflict on children's rights, including rights to education and health.

Between 2005 and 2020, the United Nations verified more than 13,900 incidents of attacks, including direct attacks or attacks where there has not been adequate distinction between civilian and military objectives, on educational and medical facilities and protected persons, including pupils and hospitalised children, and health and school personnel.

These attacks not only put children's lives at risk, but also disrupt their learning and limit their access to medical assistance, which can have a lifelong impact on their education, economic opportunities and overall health.

4. Rape or other grave sexual violence

Rape or other grave sexual violence includes acts of rape, other sexual violence, sexual slavery and/or trafficking, enforced prostitution, forced marriage or pregnancy, enforced sterilization, or sexual exploitation and/or abuse of children. In some cases, sexual violence is used to intentionally humiliate a population or to force people from their homes.

Between 2005 and 2020, parties to conflict raped, forcibly married, sexually exploited, and committed other grave forms of sexual violence against at least 14,200 children.

However, the widespread stigma around rape and sexual violence means it is a particularly under-reported issue affecting children in conflict. Sexual violence disproportionately affects girls, who were victims in 97 per cent of cases from 2016 to 2020.

5. Abduction of children

Abduction of children refers to the unlawful removal, seizure, capture, apprehension, or enforced disappearance of a child either temporarily or permanently. Whether it's an intentional act of violence or retaliation, to instill fear among populations, or to forcibly recruit and/or sexually abuse

children, abduction is one of the most pervasive violations committed against children in situations of armed conflict.

Between 2005 and 2020, at least 25,700 children were verified as abducted by parties to conflict. Boys account for three quarters of verified instances of abducted children.

However, girls remain at risk of being abducted, including for the purpose of sexual violence and exploitation. In many cases, children who are abducted are also victims of other grave violations, such as killing, maiming, sexual violence or recruitment into armed groups. They might also be held hostage or arbitrarily detained.

6. Denial of humanitarian access for children

Denial of humanitarian access for children includes the intentional deprivation or impediment of humanitarian assistance essential for children's survival by parties to the conflict, including willfully impeding the ability of humanitarian or other relevant actors to access and assist affected children in situations of armed conflict.

The United Nations verified at least 14,900 incidents of denial of humanitarian access for children between 2005 and 2020, with eighty per cent of those verified cases taking place from 2016 to 2020, underscoring enhanced efforts to document and verify these incidents. Warring parties often deny humanitarian actors access to those in need or prevent assistance from reaching civilian populations. Civilians are also denied aid when humanitarian workers are targeted and treated as threats.

Between 2005 and 2020, more than 266,000 grave violations were verified against children, committed by parties to conflict in more than 30 conflict situations across Africa, Asia, the Middle East, and Latin America. The actual number is undoubtedly far higher as access and security constraints, as well as the shame, pain and fear that survivors suffer often hamper the reporting, documentation and verification of these violations.

26 August 2021

Up to six million people: the unrecorded fatalities of the 'War on Terror'

Nafeez Ahmed examines the direct and indirect deaths of the post 9/11 era, as a new kind of state-sanctioned mass violence became globalised and normalised.

Twenty years after the 9/11 terrorist attacks, compelling statistical data has emerged suggesting that the true death toll of the 'War on Terror' could be as high as six million people – and that this colossal figure is itself likely to be conservative.

The costs of war project

Earlier this month, Brown University's Costs of War project updated its rolling analysis of the number of people killed in direct violence due to the post-9/11 'War on Terror'.

It found that just under a million people – between 897,000 and 929,000 – were killed directly due to violence across five theatres of war involving significant US and Western military involvement: Afghanistan, Pakistan, Iraq, Syria and Yemen.

These numbers have been widely reported as proving that around one million people have been killed in post-9/11 wars. Yet, they are extremely conservative figures.

The real death toll is far, far higher – a fact that has not been properly reported in media reports.

'The deaths we tallied are likely a vast under-count of the true toll these wars have taken on human life,' said the co-author of the Costs of War project report Professor Neta Crawford – noting that the tally does not incorporate indirect deaths due to the consequences of war through the destruction of civilian infrastructure.

The new figures therefore do not account for the many indirect deaths the War on Terror has caused by way of disease, displacement and loss of access to food or clean drinking water, she acknowledged.

The Geneva Declaration report concludes that we are safe to assume on average four indirect deaths to every direct death in contemporary conflicts.

An invisible death toll

The most accurate way to calculate the scale of total deaths would be through epidemiological surveys to determine 'excess deaths' by comparing pre-war and post-war mortality rates, which would encompass both direct and indirect deaths.

However, in many of these countries, the infrastructure to monitor and collect the relevant data does not exist or is very hard to obtain, which is why such surveys are rare.

In the absence of epidemiological analysis, it is still possible to develop a clear sense of the minimum likely scale of indirect deaths.

Last September, when commenting on an earlier version of the project's findings, Costs of War report co-author Professor Catherine Lutz pointed out that 'one has to

multiply that direct death number… by an estimated two to four times to get to the total number of people – in the millions – who are dead today who would not have been dead had the wars not been fought'. But even this approach is likely to produce an under-count.

According to a landmark report by the Geneva Declaration on Armed Violence and Development – signed by 113 governments – in 'the majority of conflicts since the early 1990s, for which good data is available, the burden of indirect deaths was between three and 15 times the number of direct deaths'.

The report found that, due to the impact of conflicts on public services and infrastructure, vastly greater numbers of people end up dying indirectly from the consequences of violence compared to the number that die directly from conflict.

The range varies based on different factors such as the levels of economic development in a country before a war, the duration of fighting, the intensity of combat, the population's access to basic care and services, and the success of humanitarian relief efforts.

The more intense the fighting and the more degraded the level of infrastructure, the higher the number of indirect deaths.

The report concluded that 'a reasonable average estimate would be a ratio of four indirect deaths to one direct death in contemporary conflicts'.

However, it should be noted that this ratio is a minimum average that is likely to be extremely conservative in relation to the impact of Western-backed military interventions. For instance, six months after the bombing campaign in Afghanistan in 2001, data assessed by the Guardian revealed that, although between 1,300 and 1,800 Afghans were killed directly, as many as 20,000 and possibly as high as 49,600 people had died due to the indirect consequences of the military intervention. In this case, the total number of indirect deaths was at least 15 times higher than direct deaths.

If that higher, empirically-substantiated ratio was applied to the Costs of War direct death figures in Afghanistan since 9/11 (176,000 people), it would imply 2,640,000 indirect deaths in that country to date, which would suggest that in just one country a total of about 2.8 million Afghans have been killed due to the War on Terror.

This scale of violence has been corroborated by one other assessment of avoidable mortality in Afghanistan by retired La Trobe University biochemist Dr Gideon Polya. His book, *Body Count: Global Avoidable Mortality Since 1950*, put total excess deaths of Afghans since 2001 at three million.

The very dynamics of mass violence have become globalised and normalised, precisely because our political and cultural institutions are incapable of acknowledging that such state-sanctioned terrorism even exists.

While the Geneva Declaration approach cannot be used to produce precise figures, it can provide an accurate insight into the likely order of magnitude of total deaths in a way that simple direct death figures cannot.

Applying its methodology to the Costs of War project figures suggests that the overall number of indirect deaths from 20 years of the War on Terror is between at least 3,588,000 and 3,716,000 people. This indicates that Brown University's one million figure is extremely conservative and that the total death toll is actually at least between 4,485,000 and 4,645,000 people.

Once again, these cannot be taken as specific figures, but rather as an indication of the real magnitude of deaths – likely to be a minimum of 4.5 million people. Even this estimate is highly likely to be too low, given that the real ratio could be larger than 4:1, and in Afghanistan, for instance, was 15:1 at the height of the 2001 bombing campaign.

Syria and Libya

In 2019, I was commissioned by the Hub Foundation in California to examine the available data on deaths in Muslim-majority regions as a consequence of post-9/11 conflicts. The data from that exercise suggest that some of Brown University's figures for direct deaths are almost certainly too low.

In particular, the project's estimate of the Syrian death toll is only 266,000, based on death tallies for after US intervention in 2014. The authors acknowledge that many of these deaths would also have been caused by other parties.

But as I have documented for the International State Crime Initiative at Queen Mary University of London, US and Western intervention in Syria began much earlier – as early as 2011 – and took a range of covert and overt forms which played a crucial role in igniting and prolonging the conflict in various ways.

While this does not lessen the responsibility of Syrian dictator Bashar al-Assad and his backers – Russia and Iran – in the violence, it does show that it is arbitrary to begin the death count in 2014 as if that is the pivotal date of US involvement. This means that the actual direct death toll in Syria is far higher – around some 511,000 people (according to groups both opposed to and sympathetic to Assad) – a figure which itself is probably conservative.

In addition to the five theatres of war examined by Brown University, I had also incorporated data from the NATO intervention in Libya, including some 27,361 direct deaths. When the Geneva Declaration 4:1 average ratio is applied to these figures, the numbers are sobering. My original analysis in 2019 had incorporated Brown University's older data compiled that year, but the new report shows the figures are now higher.

Below, I have incorporated Brown University's new figures to update my original analysis, along with the more accurate figures for Syria, and taking into account Libya, to develop a

range of plausible estimates of indirect deaths that should be recognised as probably conservative.

More than 5.8 million total deaths

Rather than applying the Geneva Declaration approach wholesale to the overall direct death figures, I have applied it case-by-case for each theatre of war to produce a likely order of magnitude figure for indirect deaths.

These final figures are then totalled to generate an overall cumulative death toll for each conflict zone, which in turn is used to calculate an overall estimate for the total number of deaths across all these theatres of war. As these are not precise figures, they have been rounded to the nearest thousand.

This analysis shows that the total number of direct deaths during the War on Terror in major war zones with significant involvement of Western governments amounts to around 1.2 million people.

In addition to this figure, applying the Geneva Declaration methodology suggests that between 4.2 and 4.6 million is the range encompassing the minimum number of people who are likely to have died as an indirect consequence of these post-9/11 wars.

When the number of direct and indirect deaths in each major war zone is then totalled, it reveals that at least 5.8 to 6 million people are likely to have died overall due to the War on Terror – a staggering number which is still probably very conservative.

These estimates cannot be assumed to hold with precision, but they demonstrate the real scale of the consequences of the violence inflicted.

While it is obviously not possible to attribute these deaths specifically to a particular party in the way that has been attempted with direct death tallies, these deaths are causally related to the chain of events that began with post-9/11 military policies implemented by the US, UK and other Western states.

Without that chain of events, these wars and their devastating outcomes simply would not have happened.

The nature of war

To the extent that the Costs of War project's conservative direct death tallies are widely reported and cited as a reliable indicator of the scale of violence in the War on Terror, there is a risk that the true, far higher but largely invisible, scale of death remains suppressed from public consciousness.

On 9/11, nearly 3,000 innocent Americans were killed on US soil. In the ensuing 20 years, just over one million people were directly killed in the series of wars that followed as a result. But that is only a part of the story because the one million figure is a vast under-count of the true total death toll.

In reality, it is likely that at least six million people have been killed in the course of the War on Terror, and that the vast majority of those killed are of Muslim origin.

	Direct deaths	Probable indirect deaths	Total cumulative death toll including direct and indirect deaths
Yemen	112,092	448,368	560,460
Syria	511,000	2,044,000	2,555,000
Libya	27,361	109,444	136,805
Iraq	275,087 – 306,495	1,100,348 – 1,225,980	1375,435 – 1,532,475
Afghanistan	176,000	704,000	880,000
Pakistan	67,000	268,000	335,000
	1,168,540 – 1,199,948 (1,169,000 – 1,200,000 rounded to the nearest thousand)	4,203,404 – 4,589,916 (4,203,000 – 4,590,000 rounded to the nearest thousand)	5,842,700 – 5,999,740 (5,843,000 – 6,000,000 rounded to the nearest thousand)

Yet, it is in the very nature of how these wars have been conducted that we can never be truly certain of the full scale of the deaths they have caused both directly and indirectly.

The true scale of the destruction caused by the War on Terror remains largely taboo, unreported and unexplored by most media commentators and academic experts, let alone policy-makers.

To even contemplate that such a huge number of people might have been killed as a result of decisions by US, British and European leaders – in the name of fighting terrorism – strays too far outside the framework of what is culturally acceptable and intellectually palatable. Such a scale of death is not what 'we' do. We are not 'terrorists'.

However if the true consequences of these wars are examined, we might begin to recognise how the nature of conflict and violence has transformed through the 20th and 21st Centuries. It has become imperceptible, embedded in far-flung institutions of power, upheld through short-sighted military operations with structures and ethics designed in such a way that they systematically maximise the deaths of invisible 'others' in the name of protecting 'our' more important bodies and interests.

The very dynamics of mass violence have become globalised and normalised, precisely because our political and cultural institutions are incapable of acknowledging that such state-sanctioned terrorism even exists.

Twenty years after 9/11, the shocking fact is that, due to our lack of interest as a civilisation, no one really knows for sure how many people have died as a result of the War on Terror. Now the Taliban's return to power in Afghanistan has added insult to injury, providing proof that the projection of extreme force only ever empowers more extremists.

As the Taliban stocks up its new Government with designated terrorists and as al-Qaeda accelerates its capacity to regroup, there is no longer any excuse. We need to fundamentally rethink our entire approach to what we call 'security' and re-evaluate how we have allowed ourselves to reach this point of devastation and delusion. If we don't, the return of the Taliban is merely the beginning of an untimely end.

15 December 2021

Afghanistan: war shatters bodies and souls. Four decades of war shatters nations.

The following is a statement from Peter Maurer, President of the International Committee of the Red Cross, at the end of a four-day trip to Afghanistan.

Kabul (ICRC) – The scars of war last generations. Destroyed buildings can one day be rebuilt, but shattered limbs do not regrow. Children re-live trauma long after the bomb blasts subside. Family members killed leave a permanent void.

The people of Afghanistan have lived through 40 years of conflict. In my years as the president of the International Committee of the Red Cross I have seen agony, suffering and despair in many of the world's war zones. But I cannot begin to express how deeply four decades of war damages a nation.

That's why Afghanistan's challenges are so mammoth. The good news is that humanitarian action helps stabilize society. Compassion and empathy help heal the wounds of war. Funding that ensures health care, clean water and schools can help pull Afghan families from misery's depths. It's crucial that the international community finds solutions, even if temporary, to ensure continued funding. The needs of Afghan families can't wait for the resolution of political change.

To be effective, humanitarian work must be inclusive – of women, girls and ethnic minorities. That's why the ICRC makes sure that women in Afghanistan have access to our services, including medical and rehabilitation, and we make sure we have female medical and rehabilitation staff on our teams.

I encourage authorities to continue access to health services for women – but also – access to education. In a country where only 50 per cent of women deliver in a health facility with trained staff, it's critically important that Afghanistan have more educated women midwives and doctors.

During my four-day visit to Afghanistan, I met with Mullah Baradar and other Taliban leadership. I emphasized ICRC's neutral, impartial and independent humanitarian work and noted that we have been assisting Afghans affected by conflict for more than 30 years, and that we won't stop now.

Our long history in the country tells us that Afghanistan's victims of war will need years of assistance and rehabilitation. The toll from only the most recent fighting has been huge.

More than 41,000 people wounded by war were treated at ICRC-supported health facilities from June to August, an 80 percent increase compared with the same period last year.

Quality medical care is a top concern for Afghan families. Last month the ICRC doubled the number of health facilities we support to 89 clinics and mobile health teams, up from 46, in addition to two hospitals, one in Kandahar and the other in Kabul, which is run by the Afghanistan Red Crescent Society.

We want to enhance access to immunizations and primary health care – including for pregnant women. Sadly, clinics are seeing a rise in the number of children wounded by newly laid mines. De-mining efforts must be prioritised, for

the sake of all the naturally curious children who one day soon may pick up a mine and lose a limb – or their life.

ICRC's orthopaedic services have helped more than 210,000 physically disabled patients since we began our work in Afghanistan in 1988. We see about 150,000 patients a year.

We help them walk again. Just as important, we help them reintegrate into society with dignity. My visit to our Kabul centre put a smile on my face as I watched proud and determined Afghans re-learn to walk or use a new prosthetic arm.

COVID-19 presents another major challenge. When bombs are falling and bullets flying, families do not have the luxury of worrying about masks and physical distancing. Still, COVID continues its spread. But the country hasn't received nearly enough doses of the vaccine, and I'm urging world governments to ensure it gets an equitable share.

Where did 40 years of war leave Afghan families? Some 9 out of 10 people live on less than $2 a day. Some 10 million people are experiencing high levels of food insecurity, according to the latest IPC data. Unaccompanied minors have recently been separated from their families during the crush at Kabul airport, a challenge the global Red Cross Red Crescent family will tackle, to reunite as many separated families as possible.

The world has come to know Afghanistan as a land of beauty, but also one of heart-break. War shatters bodies and souls. Four decades of war shatters nations. My greatest hope now is that we all pitch in to help the wounded to heal, the separated families to find one another again, and that any future fighting spares as many civilians as possible.

8 September 2021

War crimes

Definition from the United Nations Office on Genocide Prevention and the Responsibility to Protect.

Background

Even though the prohibition of certain behaviour in the conduct of armed conflict can be traced back many centuries, the concept of war crimes developed particularly at the end of the 19th century and beginning of the 20th century, when international humanitarian law, also known as the law of armed conflict, was codified. The Hague Conventions adopted in 1899 and 1907 focus on the prohibition to warring parties to use certain means and methods of warfare. Several other related treaties have been adopted since then. In contrast, the Geneva Convention of 1864 and subsequent Geneva Conventions, notably the four 1949 Geneva Conventions and the two 1977 Additional Protocols, focus on the protection of persons not or no longer taking part in hostilities. Both Hague Law and Geneva Law identify several of the violations of its norms, though not all, as war crimes. However there is no one single document in international law that codifies all war crimes. Lists of war crimes can be found in both international humanitarian law and international criminal law treaties, as well as in international customary law.

The 1949 Geneva Conventions have been ratified by all Member States of the United Nations, while the Additional Protocols and other international humanitarian law treaties have not yet reached the same level of acceptance. However, many of the rules contained in these treaties have been considered as part of customary law and, as such, are binding on all States (and other parties to the conflict), whether or not States have ratified the treaties themselves. In addition, many rules of customary international law apply in both international and non-international armed conflict, expanding in this way the protection afforded in non-international armed conflicts, which are regulated only by common article 3 of the four Geneva Conventions and Additional Protocol II. Definition

Definition

Rome Statute of the International Criminal Court

Article 8

War crimes

1. The Court shall have jurisdiction in respect of war crimes in particular when committed as part of a plan or policy or as part of a large-scale commission of such crimes.
2. For the purpose of this Statute, 'war crimes' means:

a) Grave breaches of the Geneva Conventions of 12 August 1949, namely, any of the following acts against persons or property protected under the provisions of the relevant Geneva Convention:

- Wilful killing
- Torture or inhuman treatment, including biological experiments;
- Wilfully causing great suffering, or serious injury to body or health;
- Extensive destruction and appropriation of property, not justified by military necessity and carried out unlawfully and wantonly;
- Compelling a prisoner of war or other protected person to serve in the forces of a hostile Power;
- Wilfully depriving a prisoner of war or other protected person of the rights of fair and regular trial;
- Unlawful deportation or transfer or unlawful confinement;
- Taking of hostages.

b) Other serious violations of the laws and customs applicable in international armed conflict, within the established framework of international law, namely, any of the following acts:

- Intentionally directing attacks against the civilian

population as such or against individual civilians not taking direct part in hostilities;

- Intentionally directing attacks against civilian objects, that is, objects which are not military objectives;

- Intentionally directing attacks against personnel, installations, material, units or vehicles involved in a humanitarian assistance or peacekeeping mission in accordance with the Charter of the United Nations, as long as they are entitled to the protection given to civilians or civilian objects under the international law of armed conflict;

- Intentionally launching an attack in the knowledge that such attack will cause incidental loss of life or injury to civilians or damage to civilian objects or widespread, long-term and severe damage to the natural environment which would be clearly excessive in relation to the concrete and direct overall military advantage anticipated;

- Attacking or bombarding, by whatever means, towns, villages, dwellings or buildings which are undefended and which are not military objectives;

- Killing or wounding a combatant who, having laid down his arms or having no longer means of defence, has surrendered at discretion;

- Making improper use of a flag of truce, of the flag or of the military insignia and uniform of the enemy or of the United Nations, as well as of the distinctive emblems of the Geneva Conventions, resulting in death or serious personal injury;

- The transfer, directly or indirectly, by the Occupying Power of parts of its own civilian population into the territory it occupies, or the deportation or transfer of all or parts of the population of the occupied territory within or outside this territory;

- Intentionally directing attacks against buildings dedicated to religion, education, art, science or charitable purposes, historic monuments, hospitals and places where the sick and wounded are collected, provided they are not military objectives;

- Subjecting persons who are in the power of an adverse party to physical mutilation or to medical or scientific experiments of any kind which are neither justified by the medical, dental or hospital treatment of the person concerned nor carried out in his or her interest, and which cause death to or seriously endanger the health of such person or persons;

- Killing or wounding treacherously individuals belonging to the hostile nation or army;

- Declaring that no quarter will be given;

- Destroying or seizing the enemy's property unless such destruction or seizure be imperatively demanded by the necessities of war;

- Declaring abolished, suspended or inadmissible in a court of law the rights and actions of the nationals of the hostile party;

- Compelling the nationals of the hostile party to take part in the operations of war directed against their own country, even if they were in the belligerent's service before the commencement of the war;

- Pillaging a town or place, even when taken by assault;

- Employing poison or poisoned weapons;

- Employing asphyxiating, poisonous or other gases, and all analogous liquids, materials or devices;

- Employing bullets which expand or flatten easily in the human body, such as bullets with a hard envelope which does not entirely cover the core or is pierced with incisions;

- Employing weapons, projectiles and material and methods of warfare which are of a nature to cause superfluous injury or unnecessary suffering or which are inherently indiscriminate in violation of the international law of armed conflict, provided that such weapons, projectiles and material and methods of warfare are the subject of a comprehensive prohibition and are included in an annex to this Statute, by an amendment in accordance with the relevant provisions set forth in articles 121 and 123;

- Committing outrages upon personal dignity, in particular humiliating and degrading treatment;

- Committing rape, sexual slavery, enforced prostitution, forced pregnancy, as defined in article 7, paragraph 2 (f), enforced sterilization, or any other form of sexual violence also constituting a grave breach of the Geneva Conventions;

- Utilizing the presence of a civilian or other protected person to render certain points, areas or military forces immune from military operations;

- Intentionally directing attacks against buildings, material, medical units and transport, and personnel using the distinctive emblems of the Geneva Conventions in conformity with international law;

- Intentionally using starvation of civilians as a method of warfare by depriving them of objects indispensable to their survival, including wilfully impeding relief supplies as provided for under the Geneva Conventions;

- Conscripting or enlisting children under the age of fifteen years into the national armed forces or using them to participate actively in hostilities.

c) In the case of an armed conflict not of an international character, serious violations of article 3 common to the four Geneva Conventions of 12 August 1949, namely, any of the following acts committed against persons taking no active part in the hostilities, including members of armed forces who have laid down their arms and those placed hors de combat by sickness, wounds, detention or any other cause:

- Violence to life and person, in particular murder of all kinds, mutilation, cruel treatment and torture;

- Committing outrages upon personal dignity, in particular humiliating and degrading treatment;

- Taking of hostages;

- The passing of sentences and the carrying out of executions without previous judgement pronounced by a regularly constituted court, affording all judicial guarantees which are generally recognized as indispensable.

d) Paragraph 2 (c) applies to armed conflicts not of an international character and thus does not apply to situations of internal disturbances and tensions, such as riots, isolated and sporadic acts of violence or other acts of a similar nature.

e) Other serious violations of the laws and customs applicable in armed conflicts not of an international character, within the established framework of international law, namely, any of the following acts:

- Intentionally directing attacks against the civilian population as such or against individual civilians not taking direct part in hostilities;
- Intentionally directing attacks against buildings, material, medical units and transport, and personnel using the distinctive emblems of the Geneva Conventions in conformity with international law;
- Intentionally directing attacks against personnel, installations, material, units or vehicles involved in a humanitarian assistance or peacekeeping mission in accordance with the Charter of the United Nations, as long as they are entitled to the protection given to civilians or civilian objects under the international law of armed conflict;
- Intentionally directing attacks against buildings dedicated to religion, education, art, science or charitable purposes, historic monuments, hospitals and places where the sick and wounded are collected, provided they are not military objectives;
- Pillaging a town or place, even when taken by assault;

- Committing rape, sexual slavery, enforced prostitution, forced pregnancy, as defined in article 7, paragraph 2 (f), enforced sterilization, and any other form of sexual violence also constituting a serious violation of article 3 common to the four Geneva Conventions;
- Conscripting or enlisting children under the age of fifteen years into armed forces or groups or using them to participate actively in hostilities;
- Ordering the displacement of the civilian population for reasons related to the conflict, unless the security of the civilians involved or imperative military reasons so demand;
- Killing or wounding treacherously a combatant adversary;
- Declaring that no quarter will be given;
- Subjecting persons who are in the power of another party to the conflict to physical mutilation or to medical or scientific experiments of any kind which are neither justified by the medical, dental or hospital treatment of the person concerned nor carried out in his or her interest, and which cause death to or seriously endanger the health of such person or persons;
- Destroying or seizing the property of an adversary unless such destruction or seizure be imperatively demanded by the necessities of the conflict;

f) Paragraph 2 (e) applies to armed conflicts not of an international character and thus does not apply to situations

of internal disturbances and tensions, such as riots, isolated and sporadic acts of violence or other acts of a similar nature. It applies to armed conflicts that take place in the territory of a State when there is protracted armed conflict between governmental authorities and organized armed groups or between such groups.

3. Nothing in paragraph 2 (c) and (e) shall affect the responsibility of a Government to maintain or re-establish law and order in the State or to defend the unity and territorial integrity of the State, by all legitimate means.

Elements of the crime

War crimes are those violations of international humanitarian law (treaty or customary law) that incur individual criminal responsibility under international law. As a result, and in contrast to the crimes of genocide and crimes against humanity, war crimes must always take place in the context of an armed conflict, either international or non-international.

What constitutes a war crime may differ, depending on whether an armed conflict is international or non-international. For example, Article 8 of the Rome Statute categorises war crimes as follows:

♦ Grave breaches of the 1949 Geneva Conventions, related to international armed conflict;

♦ Other serious violations of the laws and customs applicable in international armed conflict;

♦ Serious violations of Article 3 common to the four 1949 Geneva Conventions, related to armed conflict not of an international character;

♦ Other serious violations of the laws and customs applicable in armed conflict not of an international character.

From a more substantive perspective, war crimes could be divided into: a) war crimes against persons requiring particular protection; b) war crimes against those providing humanitarian assistance and peacekeeping operations; c) war crimes against property and other rights; d) prohibited methods of warfare; and e) prohibited means of warfare.

Some examples of prohibited acts include: murder; mutilation, cruel treatment and torture; taking of hostages; intentionally directing attacks against the civilian population; intentionally directing attacks against buildings dedicated to religion, education, art, science or charitable purposes, historical monuments or hospitals; pillaging; rape, sexual slavery, forced pregnancy or any other form of sexual violence; conscripting or enlisting children under the age of 15 years into armed forces or groups or using them to participate actively in hostilities.

War crimes contain two main elements:

♦ A contextual element: 'the conduct took place in the context of and was associated with an international/non-international armed conflict';

♦ A mental element: intent and knowledge both with regards to the individual act and the contextual element.

In contrast to genocide and crimes against humanity, war crimes can be committed against a diversity of victims, either combatants or non-combatants, depending on the type of crime. In international armed conflicts, victims include wounded and sick members of armed forces in the field and at sea, prisoners of war and civilian persons. In the case of non-international armed conflicts, protection is afforded to persons taking no active part in the hostilities, including members of armed forces who have laid down their arms and those placed 'hors de combat' by sickness, wounds, detention, or any other cause. In both types of conflicts protection is also afforded to medical and religious personnel, humanitarian workers and civil defence staff.

2021

From www.un.org/en/genocideprevention/war-crimes.shtml, by the United Nations, accessed: 24 November 2021
© 2021 United Nations.
Reprinted with the permission of the United Nations.

www.un.org

'I refuse to visit his grave': the trauma of mothers caught in Israel-Gaza conflict

Many women have lost children, been separated from newborns or are unable to breastfeed and bond with their babies because of the war.

By Stefanie Glinski *in Gaza*

In the last month of her pregnancy, May al-Masri was preparing dinner when a rocket landed outside her home in northern Gaza, killing her one-year-old son, Yasser.

Masri had felt the explosion's shockwave when the attack happened last month, but was largely unharmed. Running outside once the air had cleared, she found her husband severely wounded and her child's body covered in blood.

With her husband in a West Bank hospital – and likely to be there for months to come – Masri gave birth to a healthy boy a few weeks later. However, the trauma of the attack, and the grief of her loss, have made it difficult for the 20-year-old to bond with or breastfeed her newborn baby.

May's escalation of violence in the long-running Israel-Palestine conflict killed 256 Palestinians and 13 Israelis. Yasser was one of the 68 children killed in Gaza, according to the authorities there.

While crumbling buildings and signs of devastation can be seen throughout the small strip of land, it is the hidden impact of war, the trauma, that outweighs visible destruction.

'Trauma, stress and proximity to explosions have led to many miscarriages during the war, as well as a higher number of stillbirths,' says psychologist Helana Musleh, who works at northern Gaza's al-Awda hospital where Masri delivered her baby.

'Abnormal situations such as war can create severe fear and depression that can affect both the mother's and child's health. Hormonal changes can even prevent women from being able to breastfeed their children,' says Musleh.

Scrolling through images on her phone, Masri pulls up one of her favourites of Yasser sitting on the floor with a wide smile on his face. Tears roll down her cheeks as she strokes her fingers over the screen, her baby, Ahmad, resting on her lap, tightly wrapped in a blanket. 'I refuse to visit his grave,' she says. 'I have deleted all the photos of the explosion's destruction. I can't look at it.'

Masri has moved in with her mother; her own house was too damaged to be habitable. She gave birth in a blur, without having contractions, without producing milk for Ahmad, who is named after one of Masri's uncles, who was also killed.

'Once again, it is women and children who have been hardest hit by the latest escalation of violence in Gaza,' says Samah Kassab, a humanitarian programme officer at ActionAid who works with women such as Masri. 'We hear about new mothers unable to breastfeed or bond with their babies, and about children who are bed-wetting and unable to speak to their friends and families because of fear and anxiety.'

During 11 days of furious fighting, from 10 to 21 May, 97 women gave birth at al-Awda hospital; 31 had caesarean sections. 'Giving birth doesn't stop during war, of course, but delivering under high stress can cause complications,' says hospital director Dr Ahmad Ismail Mohanna, adding that the number of women experiencing birth difficulties remained high.

Wissam Maher Mater, 25, has still not been able to see her baby, now almost two weeks old.

'During the war, a rocket hit right outside my house, smashing our windows and doors,' Mater says. She passed out. 'From that moment on, I wasn't able to calm down any more – even once the war had stopped. I wasn't sure my baby would survive in my womb.'

After complications and a delivery by caesarean section, Mater's child was rushed to the children's hospital's intensive care unit on the other side of the city as his lungs were not strong enough to allow him to breathe unaided. Mater continues to recover in hospital herself, miles away from her baby.

'I haven't been able to see him or breastfeed him. I don't even know my child,' she says. The only assurance of his wellbeing is a photo sent to her by the nurses taking care of him – an image Mater can barely take her eyes off.

Although there is a shaky ceasefire between Israel and Hamas, many of those being cared for at al-Awda hospital fear further escalations and violence, and worry for their children's future safety.

'Even if I wanted to leave and provide my newborn son with a better future, there is no place to go,' Masri says.

30 June 2021

How Nazi war criminals lived 'mundane and untroubled lives' here in the UK

Perpetrators of some of history's worst crimes have escaped justice to live untroubled lives – but David Wilkinson hasn't forgotten them.

By Jonathan Margolis

At a courtroom near Hamburg on Thursday, a 96-year-old woman fails to appear at her trial after going on the run. As she is declared a fugitive and an arrest warrant issued, it is almost the stuff of comedy, especially as all she seems to have done was get on a metro train from her retirement home and travel a couple of stops. She is quickly apprehended.

What Irmgard Furchner stands accused of, however, is rather less amusing. She worked as a typist in a concentration camp where more than 65,000 people were murdered, around 28,000 of them Jewish. Thousands died in the camp's gas chambers. Others were clubbed to death, drowned in mud, killed by lethal injection, shot or worked to death. The allegation, which she denies, is that she knew what was going on.

At almost the same time, in a west London coffee shop, a softly spoken man is talking about the very subject of Nazis escaping justice – or in Furchner's case, if she is convicted, justice catching up with them.

'Did you know,' he says, 'that at Auschwitz, when they ran out of Zyklon B, the guards for a bit of a joke would grab newly-born babies and young children, open up the ovens and throw them in alive for the fun of hearing them scream?'

The fact that the speaker has the dark, intense eyes and big, jutting beard of a Biblical prophet, or possibly a Speakers' Corner preacher, makes even someone hardened to Holocaust stories wonder just a bit about its accuracy. But it turns out to be impeccably sourced from, among other works, a scholarly book published just last year by Mary

Fulbrook, professor of German history at University College London.

The bearded man goes on to talk, with references again, about the mass shootings of Jews in villages across eastern Europe before the concentration camps got into full killing mode, and how the massacres were watched by locals in a carnival atmosphere.

'Line after line of naked people, including women and children, thousands of them, would be shot and falling into a pit and watching it were people having a picnic, as spectators, with wine and cheese and bread and dogs running about.

'The point is,' continues the man, 'that the men who were having a lark killing babies in Auschwitz and organising – even filming – the public slaughters in those villages in almost every case got away with it and went on to have children of their own and live respectable, untroubled lives – hundreds of them here in Britain.

'Even with the current fuss about this being the 75th anniversary of the Nuremberg Trials, the appalling, shameful fact is that 99-plus per cent of those who committed what I believe to be the worst crimes in history were never even questioned about them.'

The man in the coffee shop with his chilling 'they walk among us theme' is no preacher and no mere armchair historian; he is David Wilkinson, a 65-year-old actor and film director, who has timed the cinema release of his documentary *Getting Away With Murder(s)* to coincide with both the Nuremberg Trial commemorations and, more poignantly, the moment

that the last remaining victims and perpetrators of the Holocaust are dying.

The film, which Wilkinson directs and presents, has taken him 18 years and a near six-figure sum of his savings, as well as those of his wife, Amy Roberts, costume designer for The Crown. He also called in favours from film-industry friends, including Dame Eileen Atkins, who voices some of the most shocking accounts of how nearly a million of the worst criminals in history got away unpunished or barely punished.

Wilkinson, a Yorkshireman from Horsforth, near Leeds, made one stipulation of those he invited to work on the film: that, like him, they shouldn't be Jews.

The idea came from Wilkinson's friend and dramatist Sir Ronald Harwood, who was Jewish. 'Before he died last year, Ronnie said: 'You must explain to people that you're doing it because you're angry and ashamed at the injustice, not because you've got an axe to grind.''

The result is a spellbinding film which, due to its length (more than three hours) and unremitting horror, is likely to be more the stuff of streaming services than popcorn night at the multiplex.

The criminals that Getting Away With Murder(s) concentrates on are mostly small fry, rather than the 'headline acts' like Hermann Göring and Rudolph Hess, who were dealt with at Nuremberg; but small fry guilty of unfathomably massive crimes, nonetheless – such as like Anthony Sawoniuk, who lay low for 50 years, living in a council flat in Bermondsey, south London, and who worked for 20 years as a ticket collector at London Bridge Station.

Sawoniuk, a Byelorussian collaborator, was known to have murdered 15 women whom he had ordered to undress, spraying them with a machine gun and then pushing them into pits. Sawoniuk managed to get to the UK in 1946. He retired on a pension on which he could live out the remainder of his years – but was eventually tried, in 1999, and died in prison in Norwich six years later. He was the only one of the 400-plus war criminals in Britain who was convicted.

Then there was Anton Gecas, a Lithuanian who took part in executing up to 40,000 Jews and Russian prisoners of war. He lived in the Scotland from 1947, attended Herriot Watt University and worked for the National Coal Board. He later ran a popular Edinburgh bed and breakfast. Despite the Lithuanian authorities trying to extradite him, he died in Edinburgh in 2001, unpunished, aged 85. His neighbours in the Scottish capital were Jewish.

Anton Jurczuk and Oleksa Fedoryn were two former members of the Ukrainian Self-Defence Legion – otherwise known as the 14th Waffen SS – living freely in Nottingham until they died in the early-Noughties. Jurczuk was working as an electrician.

In the same city, in the university suburb of Beeston, lives to this day Malka Levine, originally from the town of Volodymyr-Volynskyi in the Ukraine. She is one of 30 survivors of a massacre of 25,000 Jews by Jurczuk and Budzinskyj's unit. A friendly farmer had hidden her as a baby and members of her family in a hole under his barn. Yet she was unaware until interviewed for Wilkinson's film that men who were likely involved in the murder of her family and neighbours were living close by. 'Their names are clearly on duty rosters from that time,' Wilkinson says. 'She was horrified that she could have been on the bus or in the supermarket next to one of them.'

Outside Britain, there are many more stories of monsters living mundane, untroubled lives. 'Many of the Germans,' Wilkinson says, 'just moved back to their hometowns and resumed life under their own name. The notorious Dr Mengele himself travelled back from Argentina to Germany under his own name twice, stayed in his hometown and was sheltered there by nuns. It seems only the police were unaware he had returned for a visit.'

One German who didn't even bother to disappear to South America was Johanna Altvater, who had once entered a small hospital full of sick children in Levine's hometown and started throwing them from a third-floor window, killing some and severely injuring others. Another favourite game of Altvater's, says Levine, was to take a newborn baby, tear it into pieces and put it in the gutter.

Altvater was tried in 1978 and again in 1982, her defence being that she was only a secretary. She was acquitted both times and died in 2003, a week before her 85th birthday. In her hometown in Germany, she was a council youth worker.

Gustav Wagner, nicknamed 'The Beast', was the first deputy commander of Sobibor extermination camp in Poland. He ran the selection process that led to slave labour or death, where some 250,000 Jews were murdered. Sentenced to death in absentia, he escaped to Brazil. After his exposure, several extradition requests were rejected. In 1980, aged 69, he was found dead with a knife in his chest. His attorney said that he had committed suicide.

Herberts Cukurs, the 'Butcher of Riga', was a pre-war aviator and Latvian national hero who directly participated in the mass murder of more than 30,000 Latvian Jews. In one instance, in 1941, he ordered an elderly Jewish man to rape a young Jewish woman; any prisoners who looked away were personally beaten to death by Cukurs. He escaped to Brazil after the war, where the Soviets tried unsuccessful to extradite him. He was assassinated by Israeli Mossad agents in Uruguay in 1965, aged 64. But in Latvia he remains a national hero; a musical about him premiered in Liepaja in 2014.

David Wilkinson accepts that Getting Away With Murder(s) is unlikely to have a long cinema life. He also acknowledges that there is a queue of subsequent, more recent unpunished outrages in countries around the world – and that it is a lot to expect people to be knowledgeable about one from almost a century ago.

There are hundreds of Nazis with similar stories, says Wilkinson. 'But I just want people, even by simply reading about the film and not watching it, to be aware that we know the exact identities and often the addresses of the many culprits who got away with murder. And that hundreds of them lived here in the UK.'

1 October 2021

Key Facts

- Wars have been a part of human history for thousands of years, and have become increasingly destructive as industrialization and technology have advanced. (page 1)

- According to a survey by the International Institute for Strategic Studies, 60% of armed conflicts have been active for at least a decade and peace-making prospects globally are in decline. (page 4)

- Between 2001 and 2005, military contractor CEO pay jumped 108 percent on average, compared to a 6 percent increase for their counterparts at other large U.S. companies. (page 10)

- The top five Pentagon contractors paid their top executives $22.5 million on average in 2018. (page 10)

- The number of people killed in fighting worldwide has mostly declined since 2014 – if you count only those dying directly in combat. According to the Uppsala Conflict Data Program, figures through the end of 2020 show battle deaths are down from seven years ago. (page 17)

- Yemen's conflict kills more people, mostly women and young children, due to starvation or preventable disease than violence. (page 17)

- Worldwide, the number of displaced people, most due to war, is at a record high. Battle deaths may be down, in other words, but suffering due to conflict is not. (page 17)

- Some 170,000 violations against youngsters – including killing, maiming, sexual violence and child recruitment – have been verified since 2010, Unicef reports. The figure amounts to the equivalent of 45 abuses every single day for 10 years. (page 26)

- In 2020 alone, explosive weapons and explosive remnants of war were responsible for at least 47 per cent of all child casualties. Between 2005 and 2020, more than 104,100 children were verified as killed or maimed in situations of armed conflict, with more than two-thirds of these verified since 2014. (page 27)

- Between 2005 and 2020, more than 93,000 children were verified as recruited and used by parties to conflict, although the actual number of cases is believed to be much higher. (page 27)

- Between 2005 and 2020, the United Nations verified more than 13,900 incidents of attacks, including direct attacks or attacks where there has not been adequate distinction between civilian and military objectives, on educational and medical facilities and protected persons, including pupils and hospitalised children, and health and school personnel (page 27)

- Between 2005 and 2020, parties to conflict raped, forcibly married, sexually exploited, and committed other grave forms of sexual violence against at least 14,200 children. Sexual violence disproportionately affects girls, who were victims in 97 per cent of cases from 2016 to 2020. (page 28)

- Between 2005 and 2020, at least 25,700 children were verified as abducted by parties to conflict. (page 28)

- When the number of direct and indirect deaths in each major war zone is totalled, it reveals that at least 5.8 to 6 million people are likely to have died overall due to the War on Terror – a staggering number which is still probably very conservative. (page 30)

- The concept of war crimes developed particularly at the end of the 19th century and beginning of the 20th century, when international humanitarian law, also known as the law of armed conflict, was codified. (page 33)

Armed conflict

A state of war where armed force is used.

Biological warfare

Also known as 'germ warfare' biological warfare uses toxins or bacteria with intent to harm or kill.

Chemical weapons

Weapons that use deadly chemicals to hurt, maim and kill their targets. These chemicals can be in the form of a gas, a liquid or a solid and can be used over a wide area.

Civil war

A war between opposing groups of citizens within the same country.

Geneva Conventions

The Geneva conventions are four treaties plus three additional protocols established to set a standard for humanitarian conduct during war.

Genocide

The deliberate mass killing of a group of people belonging to a particular racial, political or cultural group.

Humanitarian intervention

When a state uses military force against another state whose military action is violating citizens' human rights.

Internal conflict

Conflict that takes place within a state, between government forces and one or more organised groups. Or between these groups themselves.

International Humanitarian Law

A set of rules and principles that govern armed conflict. IHL protects people who are not, or are no longer, participating in hostilities.

Nuclear weapon

An explosive device that has enormous destructive power and releases a vast amount of energy. Even a small nuclear weapon has the power to wipe out a city. Also known as Weapons of Mass Destruction (WMDs).

Peacekeeping

Actively maintaining peaceful relations between nations.

PTSD

PTSD (Post Traumatic Stress Disorder) is a mental health condition caused by frightening or distressing events.

Refugee

A person who has left their home country and cannot return because they fear that they will be persecuted on the grounds of race, religion, nationality, political affiliation or social group. In the UK, a person is offically known as a refugee when they claim asylum and this claim is accepted by the Government.

War

Armed conflict between different countries/groups.states.

War crime

A war crime is an act carried out during war-time that breaches international laws governing military conflict.

Activities

Brainstorming

- As a class, brainstorm what you know about war and conflict:

  - List the major wars that you are aware of that have occurred globally in the last century

  - List the main reasons you know of that can cause conflict

  - List the different types of warfare you are aware of and the types of weapons that might be used

  - What is meant by the term WMD?

  - Where is Ukraine?

  - What event started the 'War on Terror'?

Research

- In pairs, do some online research into US arms manufacturer Lockheed Martin. Can you find out the following:

  - The types of weapons they make

  - Who they sell their weapons to

  - Their value on the stock market.

- Conduct a questionnaire among your friends, family and peers to find out their thoughts on nuclear warfare. Ask at least five different questions, including their views on recent threats surrounding the conflict in Ukraine. Write an article showing your findings and share it with the rest of your class.

- In small groups, conduct some online research into peace-keeping organisations. Find out as much as you can about their role in conflict areas. Write a list of the biggest organisations and where they are currently deployed.

- Do you know anyone, a family member or perhaps a neighbour, who lived through World War 2? Ask them if you can talk to them about their experience and what they remember from it. Write up their recollections and share with your class.

Design

- Imagine you work for a charity that is campaigning against the recruitment of child soldiers. Design a poster highlighting your cause. Where would be the best place to display it?

- Choose an article from the book and create your own illustration highlighting the key points.

- Design a poster aimed at raising funds to support refugees fleeing a war zone. Highlight the difficulties they face and the urgent basic supplies they need just to survive. Give examples of what donated money will be spent on.

Oral

- As a class, discuss the plight of children in war-torn regions. How does their life differ from yours? What issues do they experience in their everyday lives?

- In small groups talk about reports you have seen on the news about people fleeing war zones. Make a note of what you have learnt about where refugees flee to and how they try to reach safety. Share your knowledge with the rest of the class.

- Hold a debate. Divide the class into two groups, one group arguing in favour of nuclear weapons and the other against.

Reading/writing

- Write a short definition, of a couple of sentences each, for the following terms:

  - civil war

  - revolution

  - collateral damage

- Choose an article from this book and write a summary of it. It should be roughly two paragraphs long.

- Read the article *10 Conflicts to Watch in 2022* (page 17). Select one of the conflicts covered and write your own article for your school or college magazine explaining the situation.

- Imagine you are a school-age child from London who has been evacuated to the countryside during World War 2. Write a letter to your family describing your new surroundings and telling them what you miss most about home.

Acknowledgements

The publisher is grateful for permission to reproduce the material in this book. While every care has been taken to trace and acknowledge copyright, the publisher tenders its apology for any accidental infringement or where copyright has proved untraceable. The publisher would be pleased to come to a suitable arrangement in any such case with the rightful owner.

The material reproduced in **issues** books is provided as an educational resource only. The views, opinions and information contained within reprinted material in **issues** books do not necessarily represent those of Independence Educational Publishers and its employees.

Images

Cover image courtesy of iStock. All other images courtesy Freepik, Pixabay & Unsplash.

Illustrations

Simon Kneebone: pages 10, 32 & 35. Angelo Madrid: pages 2, 13 & 27.

Additional acknowledgements

With thanks to the Independence team: Shelley Baldry, and Jackie Staines. Contributing Editor: Tracy Biram

Danielle Lobban

Cambridge, January 2022